INDUSTRY 4.0

USER GUIDE

Nicola Accialini

2021© Nicola Accialini

All Rights Reserved

Table of Contents

About the author IX

Introduction XI

PART 1: OVERVIEW 1

Chapter 1: The raise of Industry 4.0 5

1.1 With the Internet of Things on the way to the 4th industrial revolution 6

1.2 Why Industry 4.0? 10

1.3 Industry 4.0 Worldwide 31

1.4 Technologies of Industry 4.0 34

1.5 Challenges of Industry 4.0 38

Chapter 2: Impact of Industry 4.0 41

2.1 Business 42

2.2 Global Security 43

2.3 Education 45

2.4 Digital Employees 47

2.5 Environment 48

2.6 New scenarios in Industry 49

QUIZ PART 1 57

PART 2: THE KEY TECHNOLOGIES 63

Chapter 3: Autonomous Robots 67

3.1 Automated Guided Vehicles 68

3.2 Collaborative Robots (Cobots) 74

3.3 Drones 82

Chapter 4: Additive Manufacturing 88

4.1 Brief History 89

4.2 Processes and materials 92

4.3 Hybrid manufacturing processes 108

4.4 Design for Additive Manufacturing 109

4.5 Benefits & Challenges 111

4.6 Applications 114

Chapter 5: Internet of Things (IoT) 120

5.1 Introduction to Internet of Things 121

5.2 Brief History 124

5.3 Industrial Internet of Things (IIoT) 125

5.4 Cyber-Physical Systems (CPS) 126

5.5 Establishing a communication 127

5.6 IoT Protocol & Standards 129

5.7 Applications of IoT 129

Chapter 6: Augmented Reality 136

6.1 Brief History 137

6.2 How AR works 138

6.3 Hardware & Software 140

6.4 Main AR smart glasses available on the market 141

6.5 Main Challenges 143

6.6 Main Applications 145

Chapter 7: Virtual Reality 148

7.1 Brief History 149

7.2 How VR works, hardware and software 152

7.3 Main benefits, limitations and applications of VR 158

Chapter 8: Big Data Analytics 160

8.1 Brief History 161

8.2 What Big Data are 162

8.3 Types of big data and main sources................................ 163

8.4 Analytics of Big Data 167

8.5 Main Benefits of Big Data Analytics 172

8.6 Big Data Analytics requirements and challenges.......... 174

Chapter 9: The Cloud..178

9.1 Brief History 179

9.2 Benefits 180

9.3 Limitations.. 183

9.4 Service Models 184

9.5 Industrial applications of Cloud Computing................... 195

Chapter 10: Simulation...198

10.1 Introduction 199

10.2 Discrete Event Simulation 200

10.3 Process Simulation 207

Chapter 11: Horizontal & Vertical IT Systems Integration 210

11.1 Introduction 211

11.2 Horizontal IT Systems Integration................................ 214

11.3 Vertical IT Systems Integration 217

11.4 Inter-Organizational IT Systems Integration 218

Chapter 12: Cyber-security 220

12.1 Brief History 221

12.2 Top 5 most notorious cyber-attacks 222

12.3 Basic concepts 225

12.4 Defense methods 229

Chapter 13: Other Technologies 234

13.1 Smart Human Machine Interface............................... 235

13.2 The Digital Twin... 240

13.3 Blockchain 245

QUIZ PART 2 256

PART 3: THE SMART FACTORY 260

Chapter 14: The Smart Factory 264

14.1 What is a Smart Factory? 265

14.2 Key word: flexibility.. 267

14.3 Prerequisites for a Reconfigurable Manufacturing System
.... 269

v

14.4 Lean Manufacturing 273

14.5 Lean 4.0 274

14.6 Smart Factory and Lights-out manufacturing 279

Chapter 15: Smart Factory implementation 282

15.1 The 10-step process 283

15.2 Risks and associated challenges 295

15.3 Examples of Smart Factories 299

QUIZ PART 3 304

PART 4: REQUIREMENTS AND SKILLS IN DEMAND 308

Chapter 16: Digital Transformation Requirements 312

16.1 Develop a high-performance culture 313

16.2 Build Relevant Digital Capabilities 315

16.3 Attract Digital Talents 316

16.4 Develop a lifelong learning approach 317

16.5 Facilitate collaboration 319

16.6 Manage data as valuable asset 321

Chapter 17: Skills in demand 324

17.1 Hard Skills 325

17.2 Soft Skills 330

QUIZ PART 4 .... **336**

Conclusion **340**

List of References 342

List of Figures 348

List of Tables 350

About the author

Nicola Accialini is an Aerospace Engineer. After graduating from the University of Padua, he worked for some of the leading aerospace companies in international contexts. In his professional career, he has managed projects related to the development of new products and the implementation of new production technologies that in 2016 led him to take an interest in the world of Industry 4.0 and the Smart Factory.

Since June 2019 he has been living and working in Spain as a consultant and he supports companies in product and process innovation processes in the manufacturing sector.

More info: www.accialiniconsulting.com

Introduction

The concept of Industry 4.0 appeared for the first time in an article published in November 2011 by the German government that resulted from an initiative regarding a high-tech strategy for 2020. Since then, several cutting-edge technologies evolved at a very fast pace and they are promising to play a crucial role in the development of smart factories.

What are the reasons that are pushing us towards a 4th industrial revolution? What are the key technologies? How industrial countries are facing it? What are the main challenges?

This book is designed to provide managers, engineers and students with the full picture of the 4th Industrial Revolution, its implications to organisations, its technologies and their applications.

This book is divided into 4 main parts:

- **PART 1: OVERVIEW**. This section provides a general overview of the 4th industrial revolution. Do we really need a step change? What are the key technologies and the main implications on our way of producing goods? How are industrial countries facing this trend?

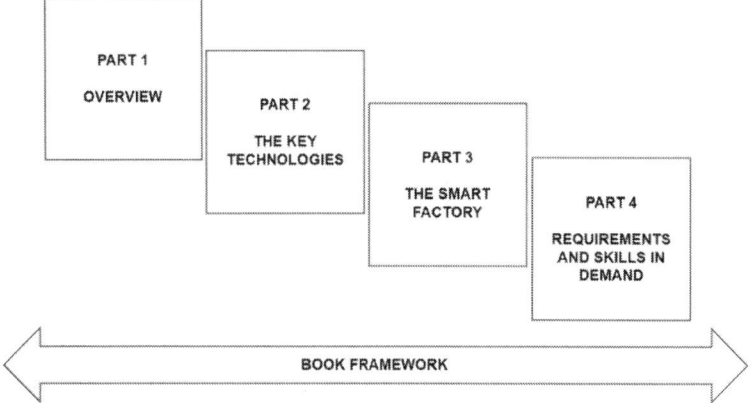

Figure 1: Book framework

- **PART 2: THE KEY TECHNOLOGIES**. In this section, we will go through a set of technologies which will be the bricks to build digital factories, the final goal of Industry 4.0. For each technology, we will provide a brief historical overview, we will explain how the technology works and what solutions are currently available on the market. Finally, we will present some concrete ideas for the implementation of pilot projects in an existing facility.

- **PART 3: THE SMART FACTORY**. In this section, we will provide a proper definition of what a Smart Factory is. Indeed, designing a Smart Factory is much more than putting some digital technologies together, just like learning a new language is much more than putting some new words together. A Smart Factory combines smart solutions to create a virtuous environment in which workers may take advantage of their cognitive skills instead of doing repetitive tasks. A step-by-step approach for the implementation of a Smart Factory will be provided, and some practical examples of existing factories will be described.

- **PART 4: REQUIREMENTS AND SKILLS IN DEMAND**. The last part of the book describes the requirements that companies must take into account if they are willing to develop new smart solutions inside their production facilities. A set of soft and hard skills will be required as well: soft skills include risk management, change management, creativity, flexibility, whereas hard skills include subjects like mechatronics, material engineering, computer technology and much more.

The content of this book is the result of a combination of extensive studies and practical experience in the aerospace industry. Several companies have been mentioned: however, it is not our intention to recommend one instead of another, but rather to provide concrete examples of off-the-shelf solutions that the market is offering now and that the reader might consider implementing.

Finally, after each part, you will have the opportunity to test your learning by taking advantage of a set of questions which will help you to develop and consolidate your 4.0 vision.

PART 1: OVERVIEW

In this first section you will learn why, where and when the concept of Industry 4.0 was developed. Moreover, main impacts on different areas of our society will be presented.

Below you will find a list of the chapters in Part 1:

Chapter 1: The raise of Industry 4.0 .... **5**

Chapter 2: Impact of Industry 4.0 .... **41**

Chapter 1: The raise of Industry 4.0

1.1 With the Internet of Things on the way to the 4th industrial revolution 6

1.2 Why Industry 4.0? 10

1.3 Industry 4.0 Worldwide 31

1.4 Technologies of Industry 4.0 34

1.5 Challenges of Industry 4.0...38

Chapter Summary

Do we need a new industrial revolution? Why 4.0?

In this first chapter, we introduce some of the key principles of Industry 4.0. First, you will be introduced to the document which made Industry 4.0 popular worldwide. After that, a brief introduction to the four industrial revolutions will be provided, focusing especially on main aspects of the third and the fourth industrial revolutions. Last, some initiatives carried out in the main industrial countries will be presented, as well as the key technologies and challenges of Industry 4.0.

Keywords: Industry 4.0, Fourth Industrial Revolution, Internet of Things, Mass Personalization, Technology

1.1 With the Internet of Things on the way to the 4th industrial revolution

The concept of Industry 4.0 appeared for the first time in an article published in November 2011 by the German government that resulted from an initiative regarding high-tech strategy for 2020. Following, the English translation of the original document[1] is reported:

"At the Hanover Fair, the initiative "Industry 4.0" will go public. Henning Kagermann, Wolf-Dieter Lukas and Wolfgang Wahlster, three representatives from business, politics and science, will show in the following article how the paradigm shift in industry will unfold. Over the next decade, new business models will become possible on the basis of cyber-physical systems. Germany could play "the first violin" here.

Being able to assert itself as a production location in a high-wage region is increasingly becoming a key issue in global competition.

In contrast to other industrialized countries, Germany has succeeded in the past ten years in keeping the number of employees in production largely stable. Not least because of the strongly medium-sized, but highly innovative

---

[1] Kagermann H., Lukas W-D., Wahlster W., Industrie 4.0: Mit dem Internet der Dinge auf dem Weg zur 4. industriellen Revolution, 2011

manufacturing industry, Germany has mastered the economic effects of the financial crisis better than many others.

The development and integration of new technologies and processes have contributed significantly to this.

To remain a production location today means getting ready for the Internet-driven fourth industrial revolution.

- *The first industrial revolution, the introduction of mechanical production equipment in the late 18th century, and*
- *The second industrial revolution, the mass production of goods by electric energy (Fordism, Taylorism) since the turn of the twentieth century, flowed from the mid-seventies into the still ongoing*
- *third industrial revolution with the further automation of production processes driven by the use of electronics and IT.*

In the field of software-intensive embedded systems, Germany has already established a leading position, especially in the automotive and mechanical engineering sectors. Now it is time to take the next step towards the Internet of Things in the industrial environment, so that Germany will become the leading provider in this new market by 2020.

The digital finishing of production plants and industrial products through to everyday products with integrated memory and communication capabilities, radio sensors, embedded actuators and intelligent software systems creates a bridge between the virtual ("cyber space") and the real world through to fine-grained synchronization between digital models and the physical reality.

The development of these cyber-physical systems in Germany already draws on the results of several successful research projects (Digital Product Memory), the aim of which is the research and use of the technology trend for innovative products and solutions.

In addition to even more industrial automation (third industrial revolution), this transformation process now includes the development of smarter surveillance and autonomous decision-making processes to control and optimize companies and entire value-added networks in near real-time.

In the industry, this approach leads to a paradigm shift in which the resulting product takes on an active role for the first time. It does not "centralize" the control, but rather the blank for a product "says" how it has to be processed in the individual production steps.

The resulting product thus controls the production process itself, monitors the relevant environmental parameters via the embedded sensors and triggers appropriate countermeasures in the event of disruptions – it simultaneously becomes the observer and the actor.

The vertical integration of embedded systems with business application software offers not only completely novel business models, but also significant optimization potential in logistics and production. The local autonomy of active digital product memories, which are installed directly at the site of events in the production and logistics chain, results in shortest reaction times in case of malfunctions and optimal use of resources in all process phases.

The products themselves thus have direct access to all higher-level process data and can "decide" in detail – while avoiding the loss of information that often occurs in centrally organized systems due to the (necessary) compression of information. This makes it possible, for example, to better meet not only the economic but also the specific ecological requirements of "green production" for a CO_2-neutral, energy-efficient city.

However, the business potential of the fourth industrial revolution lies not only in the operational process optimization, but also in their services for a variety of applications. The Internet of Things is therefore complemented by the so-called "Internet of Services" because Smart Products offer their capabilities as intelligent services. This new generation of products can independently exchange information, initiate actions and control each other via the Internet through machine-to-machine communication (M2M).

Only semantic technologies ensure the interoperability of all services based on the novel cyber-physical systems, even in open control loops.

New multimodal interaction paradigms will be needed to access the active product memories in order to make it as easy as possible for users to realize the added value of the Internet of Things and Services.

The third industrial revolution, marked by new materials, the use of robots and centralized control systems, will be replaced in the next decade with the Internet of Things based on cyber-physical systems: Germany should play the first violin here.

Therefore, the promoter group Communication of the Research Union Economy – Science of the Federal Government on January 25, 2011 proposed the future project Industry 4.0 in its recommendations for action. The future project has since been adopted, with the implementation of business, science and politics have already begun."

1.2 Why Industry 4.0?

1.2.1 The first industrial revolution (1760 – 1850)

The first industrial revolution was driven by the steam engine, patented by James Watt, a Scottish engineer, in 1769. The first applications were both for pumping water from mines and for driving machinery. The world industrial output was just 22%

between 1830 and 1860 and climbed to 42% between 1860 and 1880, mainly due to cheap steel[2].

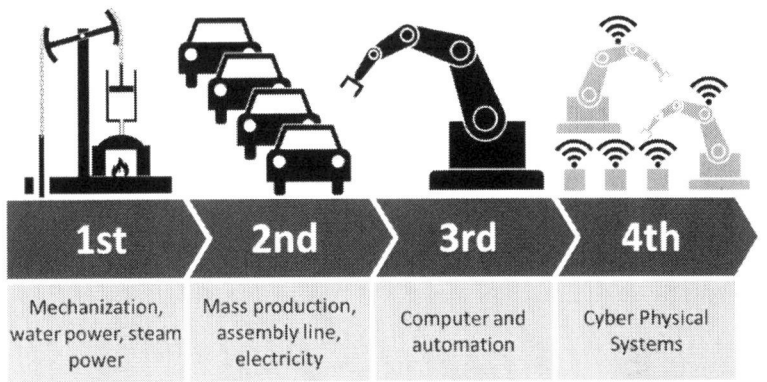

Figure 2: The Four Industrial Revolutions[3]

1.2.2 The second industrial revolution (1870 – 1914)

The second industrial revolution was driven by the electricity. Electricity, or electromagnetism, was not discovered in a single period, but was the results of different studies conducted by different people like Nikola Tesla, Benjamin Franklin, Michael Faraday, Alessandro Volta and Luigi Galvani, just to cite the most famous. However, Thomas Edison and his

---

[2] Pereira A.C., Romero F, "A review of the meanings and the implications of the Industry 4.0 concept", Procedia Manufacturing, Volume 13, 2017, Pages 1206-1214

[3] https://commons.wikimedia.org/wiki/File:Industry_4.0.png

team patented hundreds on electrical inventions, which were the basis of the Ford assembly line, the origin of mass production. World industrial output climbed 67% between 1880 and 1900[4]. The Model T, produced in 1908, is the symbol of this revolution.

1.2.3 The third industrial revolution (1950 – 1980)

The third industrial revolution was driven by computers. Although the first rudimental example was built by Charles Babbage in 1837 (the differential machine), only in the 20th century the first computers were developed, the most famous of which was the EDVAC (Electronic Discrete Variable Automatic Calculator), conceptualized by the scientist John Von Neumann in 1944, in the US. In 1947 the world's first semiconductor device was invented, while the world's first integrated circuit was patented in 1959 by Jack Kilby of the US electronics company Texas Instruments. The dawn of computers era. Computers are the basis for the development of automation, which contributes to increase the industrial productivity.

---

[4] Marsh P., The New Industrial Revolution: Consumers, Globalization and the End of Mass Production, Yale University Press publications, 2012

1.2.3.1 Science & Technology

- **Transistor:** 23 December 1947 is the birthdate of the transistor, invented by John Bardeen and Walter Brattain at AT&T's Bell Labs in Murray Hill, New Jersey. The transistor is the key active component in practically all modern electronics. Many consider it to be one of the greatest inventions of the 20th century. Its importance in today's society rests on its ability to be mass-produced using a highly automated process (semiconductor device fabrication) that achieves astonishingly low per-transistor costs.
- **Integrated circuit:** the world's first integrated circuit was described in February 1959 in a patent filed by Jack Kilby of the IS electronic company Texas Instruments. Basically, an integrated circuit is one or many circuits within a circuit. So, the most important thing of the IC is the form factor. Because it is possible to include Millions and Billions of transistors into one Germanium and silicon chip, the size of electronic devices can be reduced.
- **Microprocessor:** in 1971 the first microprocessor was unveiled. A microprocessor is a collection of circuits on a chip capable of performing like a central processing unit of a computer. The first microprocessor was made by Intel, was called 4004, and contained 2200 transistors. The 4004 had a price 95% lower than that of a comparable semiconductor chip of four year earlier.
- **Personal computer:** Although may calculators have been produced starting from the 1950s from different

companies like Olivetti in Italy, Hewlett Packard and IBM in the US, the Altair 8800 created by Micro Instrumentation and Telemetry Systems (MITS) in 1974 is considered by many to be the first true "personal computer". In 1976, Steve Jobs and Steve Wozniak sold the Apple I computer circuit board, which was fully prepared and contained about 30 chips. The Apple I computer differed from the other kit-style hobby computers of era. The first successfully mass marketed personal computer to be announced was the Commodore PET after being revealed in January 1977. During the early 1980s, home computers were further developed for household use, with software for personal productivity, programming and games. They typically could be used with a television already in the home as the computer display, with low-detail blocky graphics and a limited color range, and text about 40 characters wide by 25 characters tall. The Commodore 64, sold in total 17 million units. Another famous personal computer, the revolutionary Amiga 1000, was unveiled by Commodore on July 23, 1985. The Amiga 1000 featured a multitasking, windowing operating system, color graphics with a 4096-color palette, stereo sound, Motorola 68000 CPU, 256 KB RAM, and 880 KB 3.5-inch disk drive, for US $1,295.

- **Internet:** the origins of the Internet date back to research commissioned by the federal government of the United States in the 1960s to build robust, fault-tolerant communication with computer networks. The primary precursor network, the ARPANET, initially served as a backbone for interconnection of regional academic and military networks in the 1980s. The funding of the National Science Foundation Network as a new backbone in the 1980s, as well as private funding for other commercial extensions, led to worldwide participation in the development of new networking technologies, and the merger of many networks. The linking of commercial networks and enterprises by the early 1990s marked the beginning of the transition to the modern Internet, and generated a sustained exponential growth as generations of institutional, personal, and mobile computers were connected to the network. Although the Internet was widely used by academia since the 1980s, commercialization incorporated its services and technologies into virtually every aspect of modern life.

1.2.3.2 Socio-economic Impact

- **Globalization:** since the 1970s, aviation has become increasingly affordable to middle classes in developed countries. Open skies policies and low-cost carriers have helped to bring competition to the market. In the 1990s, the growth of low-cost communication networks cut the cost of communicating between different countries. More work can be performed using a computer without regard to location. This included accounting, software development and engineering design. Student exchange programs became popular after World War II, and are intended to increase the participants' understanding and tolerance of other cultures, as well as improving their language skills and broadening their social horizons. Between 1963 and 2006 the number of students studying in a foreign country increased 9 times.

- **Offshoring:** starting from early 1980s, due to economic expansion, there was an acceleration in plant building on a global basis. Companies could appreciate the advantages of constructing factories in the "emerging" countries whose economies were showing signs of rapid growth. By doing this, companies could both gain the benefits of lower costs and give themselves a better chance of selling products and services in these regions, as income and demand rose. For a typical product made in a country with relatively high wages, labor expenses account for 10-25% of manufacturing costs. As a result of lower ware rates elsewhere, the cost of making an item in an emerging low-cost economy may be 30-50% of the comparable amount in Western Europe, the US or Japan[5].

- **Computer revolution:** central to this revolution is the mass production and widespread use of digital logic circuits, and its derived technologies, including the computer, digital cellular phone, and the Internet. These technological innovations have transformed traditional production and business techniques. Positive aspects include greater interconnectedness, easier

---

[5] Marsh P., The New Industrial Revolution: Consumers, Globalization and the End of Mass Production, Yale University Press publications, 2012

communication, and the exposure of information that in the past could have more easily been suppressed by totalitarian regimes. The economic impact of the digital revolution has been large. Without the World Wide Web (WWW), for example, globalization and outsourcing would not be nearly as feasible as they are today. The digital revolution radically changed the way individuals and companies interact. Small regional companies were suddenly given access to much larger markets. Concepts such as On-demand services and manufacturing and rapidly dropping technology costs made possible innovations in all aspects of industry and everyday life.

- **Digital economy:** Digital economy refers to an economy that is based on digital computing technologies, although we increasingly perceive this as conducting business through markets based on the internet. The Digital Economy is worth 3 trillion dollars today. This is about 30% of the S&P 500, six times the U.S annual trade deficit or more than the GDP of the United Kingdom. What is impressive is the fact that this entire value has been generated in the past 20 years since the launch of the Internet. It is widely accepted that the growth of the digital economy has widespread impact on the whole economy. The Digital Economy uses a tenth of the world's electricity and the move to the cloud has also caused the rise in electricity use and carbon emissions. For example, a server room at a data center can use, on average, enough electricity to power 180,000 homes. The Digital Economy can be used for mining Bitcoin which, according to Digiconomist, uses an average of 70.69 TWh of electricity per year. The number of households that can be powered using the amount of power that bitcoin mining uses is around 6.5 million in the US.

1.2.3.3 Productivity

The increasing productivity is the core of every industrial revolution. As shown in Figure 3, in the last few years also productivity started to slow down together with the economic growth. Indeed, productivity can be considered the most important determinant factor of long-term economic growth. Before the financial crisis that began in 2008, the global economy was growing by about 5% a year, but currently it seems to be stuck at a growth rate lower than the postwar average, about 3-3.5% a year[6].

---

[6] Schwab K, The Fourth industrial Revolution, Portfolio Penguin, 2016

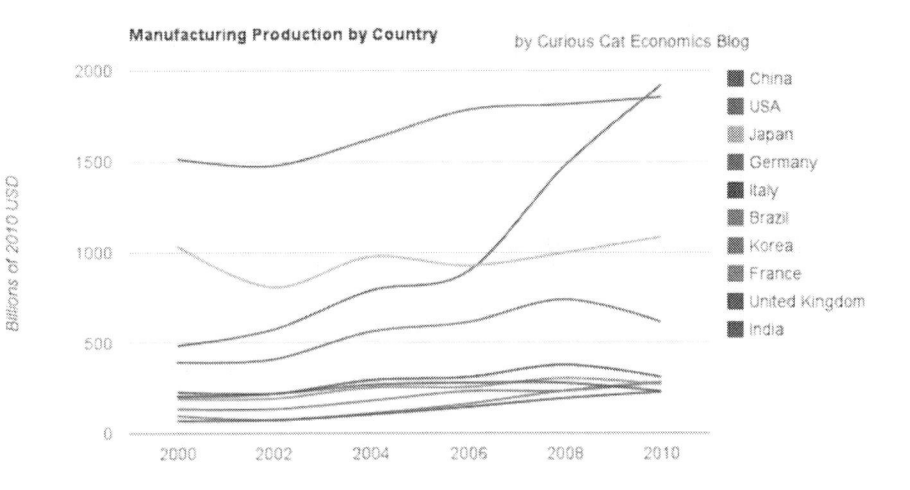

Figure 3: Manufacturing Production by Country[7]

---

[7]https://investing.curiouscatblog.net/2011/12/28/chart-of-manufacturing-output-from-2000-to-2010-by-country/

1.2.3.4 Employment

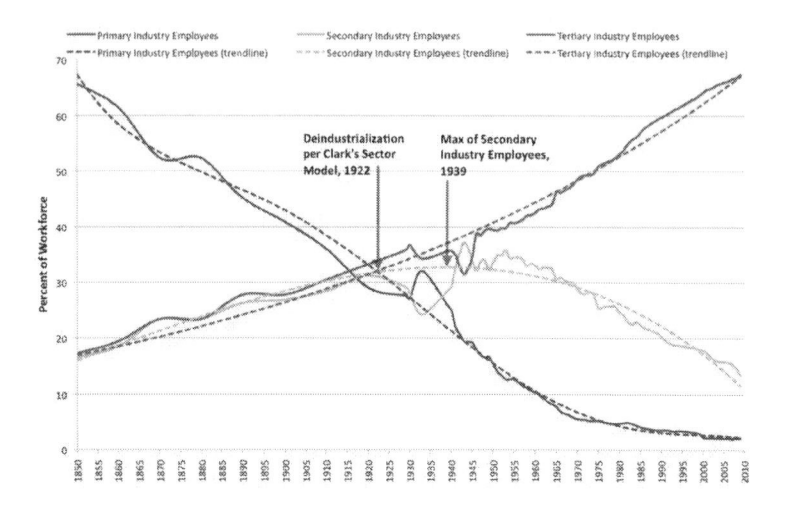

Figure 4: Clark's sector Model in the US[8]

Despite the increase of productivity, employment constantly decrease since 1945. Clark's sector model in Figure 4 shows that in the US the peak of Industry employees was between 1940 and 1945 (World War II) and then started to decline for several reasons, mainly three:

- offshoring
- technology

---

[8] https://it.m.wikipedia.org/wiki/File:Clark%27s_Sector_model.png

- finance

Marsh provides the following data: between 1900 and 1980, manufacturing employment in rich countries rose to reach 71.5 million, but from 1980 employment dropped to 63.9 in 2000 (-7.5 million) and 51.1 million in 2010 (-12.8 million)[9].

It has always happened that technological innovation destroys some jobs. Agriculture is an easy example: in the US, at the beginning of the 19th Century, people working on the land consisted of 90% of the workforce, but today, this accounts for less than 2%[10].

Figure 5 show another interesting fact: despite the fact that productivity has continued to grow over the years, however, the average hourly compensation of a US worker has not increased at the same pace. The main consequence of this is the loss of purchasing power by the American middle class and consequent crisis of the consumer society as we know it.

---

[9] Marsh P., The New Industrial Revolution: Consumers, Globalization and the End of Mass Production, Yale University Press publications, 2012
[10] Schwab K, The Fourth industrial Revolution, Portfolio Penguin, 2016

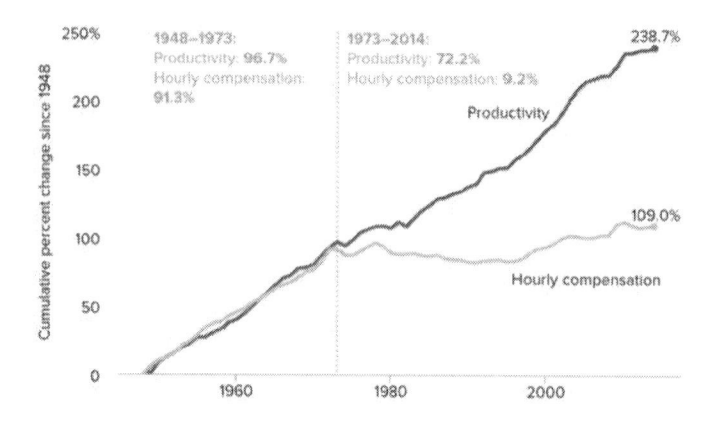

Figure 5: Disconnect between productivity and typical worker's compensation from 1948 to 2014 in the US[11]

1.2.4 The 4th Industrial Revolution (2011 – today)

"The Fourth Industrial Revolution is still in its nascent state. But with the swift pace of change and disruption to business and society, the time to join in is now"
Gary Coleman

According to Pereira et al.: *"the Industry 4.0 concept is an umbrella term for a new industrial paradigm that embraces a set of future industrial developments regarding Cyber-Physical Systems (CPS), Internet of Things (IoT), Internet of Services*

---

[11] https://www.forbes.com/sites/timworstall/2016/10/03/us-wages-have-been-rising-faster-than-productivity-for-decades/#43540eac7342

(IoS), Robotics, Big Data, Cloud Manufacturing and Augmented Reality"[12]

The 2008 financial crisis has been considered by many economists to have been the worst financial crisis since the Great Depression of the 1930s. Excessive risk-taking by banks such as Lehman Brothers helped to magnify the financial impact globally. Massive bail-outs of financial institutions and other palliative monetary and fiscal policies were employed to prevent a possible collapse of the world financial system. The crisis was nonetheless followed by a global economic downturn, the Great Recession. The European debt crisis, a crisis in the banking system of the European countries using the euro, followed later.

1.2.4.1 Socio-economic impact

For people working in the cloud, the main benefits reside in the freedom of mobility, more flexibility, the possibility of working in different places (e.g. home office), less stress and greater job satisfaction. However, it is also necessary to recognize and manage the negative impacts it can have, particularly with regard to:

- unemployment

---

[12] Pereira A.C., Romero F, "A review of the meanings and the implications of the Industry 4.0 concept", Procedia Manufacturing, Volume 13, 2017, Pages 1206-1214

- inequality
- labor markets

"Digital is the main reason just over half of the companies on the Fortune 500 have disappeared since the year 2000"
Pierre Nanterme, CEO of Accenture

According to Professor Schwab[13], the evidence is that the fourth industrial revolution seems to be creating fewer jobs in new industries than previous revolutions and that about 47% of total employment in the US is at risk, perhaps over the next decade or two. Moreover, the trend is clear: employment will grow in high-income cognitive jobs, but it will greatly diminish for routine and repetitive jobs. At the same time, this big change will force us to reconsider what we mean by "high skill". Traditionally, skilled labor means the presence of advanced or specialized education and a set of well-defined capabilities within a specific profession. However, due to the increasing rate of change of technologies, the fourth industrial revolution will place more emphasis on the ability of workers to adapt continuously and learn new skills within different contexts.

Luigi Franco[14], an Italian journalist, highlighted some key points. Martin Ford, a Silicon Valley entrepreneur and author of Rise of the Robots, sentenced that *"It will be more difficult*

---

[13] Schwab K, The Fourth industrial Revolution, Portfolio Penguin, 2016
[14] Franco L, Arrivano i robot e non solo in fabbrica. Ecco che cosa dovremmo fare perchè non ci rubino il lavoro, from FQ Millennium Magazine, Nov 2017

to automate the work of a caretaker than of a radiologist". In fact, the experience that for a radiologist requires years of studies and practice, can be collected in few minutes by a robot, once that millions of data (radiographs and reports) have been provided to him. At that point, thanks to the progresses in Imaging Recognition and AI, a machine can associate the radiograph with the right prognosis.

Another example has been reported by Marco Romandini[15]: the 24th of September 2017 in Shenzhen, China, the forum "2017 Artificial Intelligence and Mode Innovation-Legal Service Industry Reform" has been placed. The protagonist was Eva, a legal robot created by Shenzhou Yunhai Company. If robots will do most of our jobs, humans should work less, if we will still have a job. Therefore, who will provide us enough money to survive, or to buy products?

Bill Gates, founder of Microsoft, noted that *"if a human being earns 50 k$ per year working in a factory, he must pay taxes. If a robot does the same amount of job (or more), it should be taxed at the same level"*. However, this proposal has been already rejected by the European Parliament in February 2017 and has been evaluated as a nonsense by the academic world: *"If west countries introduced such a taxation, all other countries who won't tax robots will have a huge benefit, including China"*.

---

[15] Romandini M, Condannato da un legale che sembra un tostapane, from FQ Millennium Magazine, Nov 2017

Similar to the radiologist example, robots, through data collection and Machine Learning, are able to collect millions of laws, regulations and similar case studies. As you can imagine, a human can't do better.

In finance, managers, brokers and traders are under attack. In fact, a robot can calculate all variable that can influence the Stock Exchange, 24h a day, without coffee break, lunch break and any source of destruction. Goldman Sacks is moving to AI with the development of Kensho trading platform, taking example from De Shaw, Citadel and Two Sigma which are improving their performances thanks to the trading algorithm.

As we can see, there are plenty or job activities that can be automated by mean of new technologies. Even some high-skills jobs are under attack, like doctors and lawyers. The 4th industrial revolution is going to change the concept of high-skill jobs.

How to survive these scenarios?

An option could be increase salaries reducing working hours: in fact, currently there is a gap between the raise of productivity and the flatness of salaries. Another option could be the introduction of a Universal Income, which will bring to a huge social impact and transformation. Elon Musk says Universal Basic Income *"is going to be necessary"*[16].

---

[16]https://www.businessinsider.com/elon-musk-universal-basic-income-2017-2

Industry 4.0 will change the paradigm of traditional factory, enabling workers to develop high-skills that can't be substituted (so far) by robots and AI. Benefits will be a reduction in working hours, better salaries and more free time to spend in better ways than just work. The main concern then will be: how people are going to spend the massive amount of free time that they will have? This is probably the biggest challenge that smart factories will bring. People might feel useless, get to depression if the amount of free time will not be substituted properly.

It has never happened in the history that a massive amount of people is going to have such an amount of free time, therefore consequences will be unpredictable.

1.2.4.2 Production Approach

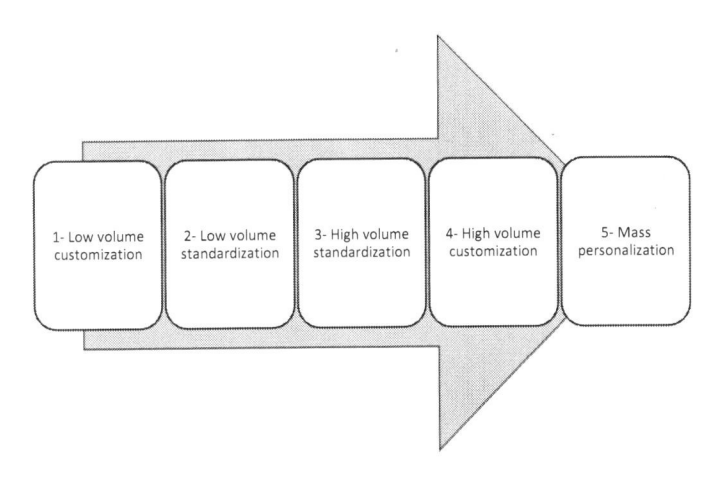

Figure 6: The five stages of production

In his book "The New Industrial Revolution" [17], Peter Marsh identifies 5 different phases:

1. The pre-industrial era has been characterized by the so-called **low volume customization**:

   "It involved the first rudimentary processes to make products from other materials such as wood, clay and metals. For the sake of simplicity, this era can be said to have started with the beginning of the Iron Age. It lasted for nearly 3,000 years, until roughly 1500 CE"

2. With the 1st industrial revolution, the **low-volume standardization** starts:

   "Helped by advances in energy transfer linked to steam engines, the first revolution lead to large factories making goods according to standardized designs and production methods. It made possible fairly simple products, using relatively large number of people. It was the major force turning agrarian-based communities into industrial ones"

3. The next phase is called **high-volume standardization**:

---

[17] Marsh P., The New Industrial Revolution: Consumers, Globalization and the End of Mass Production, Yale University Press publications, 2012

"In 1910, Ford Motor Company built the world's first mass production plant, in Highland Park, a suburb of Detroit. The factory used the system of interchangeable parts, introduced for making standard products but in large numbers. It was the start of 'high-volume standardization' – the third key stage for manufacturing processes. The period lasted from 1900 to 1980"

4. The **high-volume customization** started in parallel with the third industrial revolution:

"High-volume customization is also sometimes referred to as 'lean production', or 'mass customization' [...] Lean production employs 'teams of multi-skilled workers at all levels of the organization and [uses] highly flexible, increasingly automated machines to produce volumes of products in enormous variety. [...] The principles of the new type of manufacturing process were first applied, as with high-volume standardization, to the car. [...] The company that did most to establish the principles of high-volume customization was Toyota, now the world's biggest car-maker"

5. The current phase is called **mass personalization**:

"The fifth stage in the evolution of manufacturing processes is 'mass personalization'. The concept pushes

the idea of variation a step further than in high-volume customization. High-volume customization – of which the Toyota Production System is the best-known example – is aimed at creating products according to a range of customer tastes and requirements. However, the process is rarely used to make products so special that they are unique. The difference between high-volume customization and mass personalization is one of nuance [...] Mass personalization has many overlapping characteristics with high-volume customization, with the features of the latter taken to more extreme lengths"

As competition increases, mass personalization allows companies to offer more variations at lower cost. In this scenario, high-cost countries are likely to play a more important role. Global manufacturing towards emerging economies brought to cut production costs in high-cost countries, while their output has declined. Now the trend towards greater customization will be beneficial to many manufacturing businesses in high-cost nations. As result, companies will need to respond quickly to demands for customers for product changes This will require more of the production steps for personalization to be undertaken close to the customer. This will increase the likelihood of more product tailoring to be done in these parts of the world.

Last aspect is that key technologies to achieve mass personalization are complex, involving a mix of automation with craft skills. Development of these technologies is likely to be done in main industrialized nations.

1.3 Industry 4.0 Worldwide

Based on what happened in Germany, starting 2011 other countries proposed similar plans for their national industries.

- **Manufacturing USA**: the National Network for Manufacturing Innovation (NNMI), also known as Manufacturing USA, is a network of research institutes in the United States that focuses on developing manufacturing technologies through public-private partnerships among U.S. industry, universities, and federal government agencies. Modeled similar to Germany's Fraunhofer Institutes, the network currently consists of 14 institutes.

- **Industrie du Futur**: the programme was launched by the French government in April 2015 and aims to support companies to deploy digital technologies as well as to modernize production practices. Industrie du Futur targets selected priority markets and comprises five pillars, respectively cutting-edge technologies, business transformation, training, international cooperation and promotion of Industrie du Futur.

- **Piano Nazionale Industria 4.0**: this is the Italian's response to Industry 4.0, with an investment of more than 15 billion euro between 2017 and 2020. The plan includes the creation of highly specialized competence centers to develop the key technologies and economic incentives to support companies' investments. The Competence Centres are based in Torino, Milano, Bologna, Pisa, Padova, Napoli, Roma, Genova.

- **Industria Conectada 4.0**: it was announced in 2014 aiming at digitizing and enhancing competitiveness of Spain's industrial sector. The initiative equally seeks to provide a strategy to support companies in their digital transformation. Despite initial set-up as a public and private partnership, Industria Conectada 4.0 is driven by the General Secretary of Industry and SME. Next to the main industrial players, also experts belonging to tech companies, research and civil society are involved in Industria Conectada 4.0.

- **Catapult centres**: Catapult centres are organisations set up from 2011 onwards by Innovate UK in the United Kingdom to promote research and development through business-led collaboration between scientists and engineers to exploit market opportunities. They receive grants from public funds but are also expected to seek commercial funding.

- **Society 5.0**: Japan has its particular challenges and just as Industry 4.0 is the digital transformation of manufacturing, Society 5.0 aims to tackle several challenges by going far beyond just the digitalization of the economy towards the digitalization across all levels of the Japanese society and the (digital) transformation of society itself. Society 5.0 anticipates impacts of Industry 4.0.

- **Made in China 2025**: the goals of Made in China 2025 include increasing the Chinese-domestic content of core materials to 40% by 2020 and 70% by 2025. The Center for Strategic and International Studies describes it as an "initiative to comprehensively upgrade Chinese industry" directly inspired by the German Industry 4.0. It is an attempt to move the country's manufacturing up the value chain and become a major manufacturing power in direct competition with the United States.

The trend is clear: governments and industries in both developed and developing countries understood the potential of Industry 4.0 disruption and are planning to invest resources in this sense. The goal of developed countries is to keep manufacturing in house and to bring back home offshoring companies, while developing economies aim to keep their economic advantage through the combination of low wedge and high technology.

1.4 Technologies of Industry 4.0

How to implement Industry 4.0? We learned that Industry 4.0 is a collection of technologies, mainly digital. Nine technology trends form the building blocks of Industry 4.0, according the Boston Consulting Group (BCG).

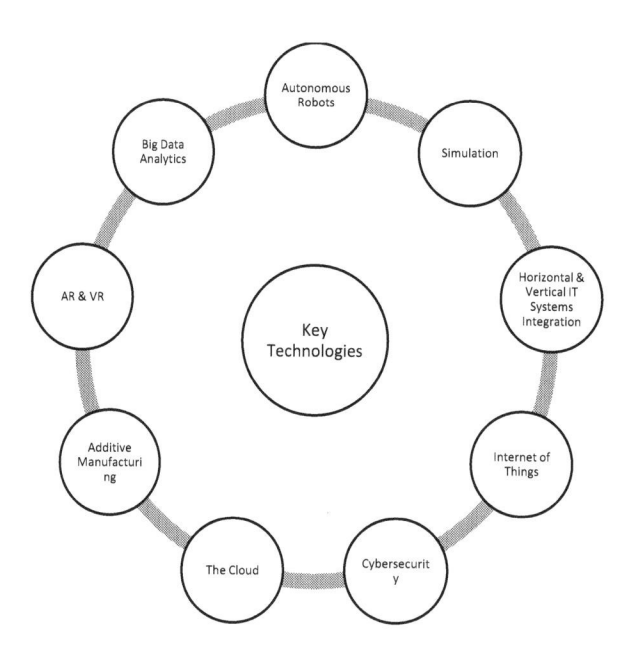

Figure 7: The 9 Key Technologies, according BCG

1. **Simulation:** simulation will be used more extensively in plant operations to leverage real-time data and mirror the physical world in a virtual model, which can include machines, products, and humans. This will allow operators to test and optimize the machine settings for the next product in line in the virtual world before the physical changeover, thereby driving down machine setup times and increasing quality.
2. **Internet of Things:** the Internet of things (IoT) is the network of physical devices, vehicles, home appliances, and other items embedded with electronics, software, sensors, actuators, and connectivity which enables these things to connect, collect and exchange data. IoT involves extending Internet connectivity beyond standard devices, such as desktops, laptops, smartphones and tablets, to any range of traditionally dumb or non-internet-enabled physical devices and everyday objects. Embedded with technology, these devices can communicate and interact over the Internet, and they can be remotely monitored and controlled. With the arrival of driverless vehicles, a branch of IoT, i.e. the Internet of Vehicles starts to gain more attention. Massive improvements in the supply chain, more transparency and visibility are guaranteed.
3. **Augmented & Virtual Reality:** augmented-reality-based systems support a variety of services, such as selecting parts in a warehouse and sending repair instructions over mobile devices. These systems are currently in their infancy, but in the future, companies will make much broader use of augmented reality to provide workers with

real-time information to improve decision making and work procedures. At the same time, Virtual Reality (VR), which is an interactive computer-generated experience taking place within a simulated environment, is promising to enhance people engagement for professional training and reduce risks in product/process development by providing a virtual experience before Capex.
4. **Additive Manufacturing:** companies have just begun to adopt additive manufacturing, aka 3D printing, which is mostly used to prototype and produce individual components. With Industry 4.0, these additive-manufacturing methods will be widely used to produce small batches of customized products that offer construction advantages, such as complex, lightweight designs.
5. **Horizontal & Vertical Systems Integration:** with Industry 4.0, companies, departments, functions, and capabilities will become much more cohesive, as cross-company, universal data-integration networks evolve and enable truly automated value chains.
6. **Big Data Analytics:** a big amount of data can be collected with digitalization of products and services. This set of data can be analyzed to predict the market trends, to improve a manufacturing process and to assess supply chain performance.
7. **Autonomous robots:** robots will interact with one another and work safely side by side with humans and learn from them. These robots will cost less and have a greater range of capabilities than those used in manufacturing today.

Example: Amazon is developing drones to deliver products.

8. **The Cloud:** more production-related undertakings will require increased data sharing across sites and company boundaries. At the same time, the performance of cloud technologies will improve, achieving reaction times of just several milliseconds. As a result, machine data and functionality will increasingly be deployed to the cloud, enabling more data-driven services for production systems. Data can be shared alla round the world, global teams can be managed virtually with less cost.

9. **Cyber-security:** with the increased connectivity and use of standard communication protocols that come with Industry 4.0, the need to protect critical industrial systems and manufacturing lines from cybersecurity threats increases dramatically. As a result, secure, reliable communications as well as sophisticated identity and access management of machines and users are essential.

1.5 Challenges of Industry 4.0

In his paper "The smart factory and its risks"[18], Frank Herrmann summarizes the main challenges within a Smart Factory:

1. **Standardization**: implementation of Industry 4.0 implies the use and connection of different IT systems from different companies with different standards. Standardization would substantially simplify connectivity of different IT systems.
2. **Cyber-security**: since Industry 4.0 is based on data generation, sharing and analysis, data is often referred to as the "raw material of the 21th century". In recent years, cyber-attacks against companies and private individuals have increased steadily. Estimates of the total annual cost to business of cyber-attacks are of the order of $500 billion[19]
3. **Availability of IT Infrastructure**: the increased use of software and networked machines and systems increases companies' dependence on a powerful, scalable and available IT infrastructure.
4. **Availability of high-speed and reliable Internet**: the "always connected" state becomes absolutely a must.

---

[18] Herrmann F, The Smart Factory and its risks, Systems 2018, 6, 38; doi:10.3390/systems6040038
[19] Schwab K, The Fourth industrial Revolution, Portfolio Penguin, 2016

5. **Complexity increase**: systems become more complex and technology evolves at a very fast rate. Keeping up with this technology will become a big challenge.
6. **Organizational risks**: since Industry 4.0 will introduce new methodologies, sometimes disruptive, people must adopt to the new approach. Therefore, it will become essential to develop change management techniques and new organizational models.
7. **Financial risks**: investments in the Industry 4.0 context are currently still rather low. This happens because management and employees are usually not properly skilled and therefore new opportunities are not easy to identify.
8. **New skills**: as already mentioned, new technologies require new skills. People should be trained at all company levels, both in horizontal and vertical direction, for 2 main reasons:
    a. being able to identify new opportunities
    b. being able to use new technologies.

    Internal training and further education ensure that the production employees are at the cutting edge of the technology.

Chapter 2: Impact of Industry 4.0

2.1 Business 42

2.2 Global Security 43

2.3 Education 45

2.4 Digital Employees 47

2.5 Environment 48

2.6 New scenarios in Industry 49

Chapter Summary

How does Industry 4.0 impact on our lives?

In this second chapter, we will provide a quick overview about main impacts of Industry 4.0 on our society from different perspectives: new business opportunities, new threats in terms of global security, new solutions to be exploited in education, new way of working with digital tools, more environmentally friendly technologies and a different approach in the industrial environment.

Keywords: business opportunities, cyberwar, elearning, digital employees, cloud, smart factory, smart product development

2.1 Business

Technologies that support the Fourth Industrial Revolution will have a big impact on how businesses are led and organized. An evidence is the average life span of a corporation listed on the S&P 500 has dropped from around 60 to approximately 18. Another evidence is the time needed by new entrants to dominate the market: Facebook took 6 years to reach revenue of $1 billion/year, and google 5 years.

The 4th industrial revolution will affect business in 4 ways:

1. **Customer Expectations:** customers are at the center of the digital economy, and potential customers can be identified based on their willingness to share data and interact. Shifting from ownership to shared access will be necessary. The digital era is moving towards accessing and using data, rather than owning goods. Car sharing schemes proposed by Uber, or BMW with Drive Now are just a practical example of business models based on sharing goods rather than ownership.
2. **Data will be a valuable asset:** Big Data Analytics are transforming the role of production and maintenance. Sensors will provide constant monitoring, providing instant feedback, sometimes by using Artificial Intelligence. On aircrafts, for example, the airline control centers inform the pilots if engines are developing a fault, and they can instruct the pilots on which countermeasures must be taken in advance.

3. **New forms of collaboration:** businesses that apparently don't have nothing to share, now are going to create partnerships and collaborations. The decision by Apple and Google to enter the automotive market shows that a tech company can now transform into a car company.
4. **New operating models** are being transformed into new digital models. An important operating model enabled by the network effects of digitalization is the platform. The platform strategy is both profitable and disruptive. Platform strategies are shifting many industries from focusing on delivering services rather than selling products. Data-driven operating models are also changing core business on well-established companies. The best example in this sense is probably Google. Google was born as a search engine company, while now its main business is selling data. According to Investopedia the bulk of Google's $110.8 billion revenue in 2017 came from its proprietary advertising service, Google AdWords[20].

2.2 Global Security

Cyber warfare is one of the most serious threats of our time. Since digital capabilities are nowadays highly

---

[20] https://www.investopedia.com/articles/investing/020515/business-google.asp

widespread (weapons, sensors, data sharing, communication and decision-making capability), no modern opponent would resist the temptation to disrupt or destroy them. This means that the distinction between war and peace will not be clear anymore, because any networks or connected devices, from military systems to civilian infrastructure such as energy sources, electricity grids, health or traffic controls, or water supplies, can be hacked or attacked. Cyber warfare can take many different forms, from criminal acts ending up to destructive attacks. Future conflicts will be transformed by the deployment of military robots and AI-powered automated weaponry:

- **drones**: they are flying robots used for a wide range of applications, from remote sensing to bombing
- **wearable devices**: these include exoskeletons which allow humans to carry high-payloads with low effort
- **additive manufacturing**: the military supply chain can be revolutionized by enabling replacements parts to be manufactured in the field from digitally transmitted design and locally available materials
- **the cloud**: through the use of social media, propaganda can be much more effective. For example, ISIS can recruit people and organize attach worldwide with very low efforts.

Personal 3D Printers could be used to duplicate keys or to print all kinds of weapons or parts of weapons. In May 2013 Cody Wilson, a law student, successfully fabricated a 3D printed single use plastic gun, and he also made 3D files for his "Liberator" weapon freely available online. The file was downloaded over 100000 times before it was blocked. Not only 3D plastic or plastic composite guns can get in the wrong hands, but they would not be detectable with a metal detector. After the aforementioned event, in December 2013 the US House of Representatives voted to extend the Undetectable Firearms Act, so banning any weapon that can evade a metal detector.

2.3 Education

We can describe changes in education from two different perspectives:

- **New skills in demand:** Professor Schwab reported some results of the Future of Jobs report conducted by the World Economic Forum report, where they asked the chief human resources officers of today's largest employers in 10 industries and 15 economies to imagine the impact on employment and skills up to the year 2020. Complex problem solving, social and systems skills will be far more in demand than content skills[21]. Giving the increasing rate of change of technologies, the fourth industrial revolution will demand and place more emphasis on the ability of

---

[21] Schwab K, The Fourth industrial Revolution, Portfolio Penguin, 2016

workers to adapt continuously and learn new skills and approaches within a variety of contexts.
- **New learning approaches:** In the last years, MOOC became popular and attractive. MOOC stands for Massive Open Online Course and it is an online course aimed at unlimited participation and open access via the web. In addition to traditional course materials such as filmed lectures, readings, and problem sets, many MOOCs provide interactive courses with user forums to support community interactions among students, professors, and teaching assistants as well as immediate feedback to quick quizzes and assignments. MOOCs are a recent and widely researched development in distance education which were first introduced in 2006 and emerged as a popular mode of learning in 2012. Main benefits include:
    - **Environmentally friendly**: travels are not required;
    - **Cost effective**: normally cheaper than standard face-to-face trainings and courses as non-core costs are eliminated;
    - **Interactive**: quizzes, forums, videos, hyperlinks and video chats can be used to improve effectiveness of learning;
    - **Self-paced learning**: Learners are able to go at their own pace and even participate in courses. No scheduling is involved.

2.4 Digital Employees

Digital economy refers to an economy that is based on digital computing technologies, although we increasingly perceive this as conducting business through markets based on the internet. The Digital Economy is worth 3 trillion dollars today. This is about 30% of the S&P 500, six times the U.S annual trade deficit or more than the GDP of the United Kingdom. What is impressive is the fact that this entire value has been generated in the past 20 years since the launch of the Internet.

The growth of Virtual Teams: Virtual Teams are made by people located in different buildings, cities, countries or continents. They may be part of the same organization or they may come from different companies. Virtual teams communicate through digital technologies, using the cloud:

1. they have virtual meeting by using web conferences and calls (e.g. Skype, Webex and similar)
2. they share files through file sharing platforms
3. they might organize face-to-face meeting periodically for workshops and assessment

With the rise of Globalization and Offshoring, virtual teams are becoming a necessity, but they imply also some benefits:

- expertise from different places can be shared
- non value-added cost can be minimized or even eliminate (travel costs)

- they are environmentally friendly, as travels are reduced or even cut out and associated pollution is eliminated.

2.5 Environment

Cloud computing has the potential to reduce a huge amount of gas emission. The world's data centres already have about the same carbon footprint as the airline industry.[22]

Compared to in-house or desktop computing, cloud computing uses server providers which can run their infrastructure more efficiently. With about half of the energy used by a large data centre going into cooling, putting cloud server farms in very cold countries would be a wise choice, saving money and carbon footprint. In preparation for its anticipated cloud computing "cold rush", Iceland is laying high-capacity, fiber optic cables to connect the country with North America and Europe.

Other beneficial impacts on Environment provided by the 4th industrial revolution are:

- use of virtual teams, as travels are reduced or even cut out

---

[22] Barnatt C, A Brief Guide to Cloud Computing: An essential guide to the next computing revolution. (Brief Histories) Little, Brown Book Group. Kindle Edition, 2010

- use of paperless work instructions, as paper usage is eliminated
- use of 3D printing, as transportation of goods will be reduced
- as previously mentioned, thanks to the Internet of Things (IoT) and intelligent assets, it is now possible to reduce greenhouse gas emissions by 9.1 billion tons by 2020, representing 16.5% of projected total in the year
- proponents of the Internet of Things and Industry 4.0 have identified energy efficiency as a significant potential benefit. The American Council for an Energy Efficiency Economy estimated potential savings of 12 to 22 percent of all energy consumed, while the consultant McKinsey suggests 10 to 20 percent energy savings

2.6 New scenarios in Industry

By definition, Industry 4.0 will have an enormous impact on organizations, mainly on manufacturing industries. In this section we are going to cover topics like

- Supply Chain
- Intellectual property
- Hybrid Manufacturing
- Work Environment
- Work organization

Supply Chain: thanks to the Internet of Things (IoT) and smart assets, it is now possible to track materials and energy flows adding more efficiency long the value chains. For example, Cisco estimated that $ 2.7 trillion can be gained from elimination of waste and improved processes in supply chains and logistics, and greenhouse gas emissions can be reduced by 9.1 billion tons by 2020, representing 16.5% of projected total in the year[23].

Intellectual Property: Intellectual Property (IP) is a category of property that includes intangible creations of the human intellect. Intellectual Property Rights is a strategic tool which is used by companies for different reasons:

- to protect innovative and profitable solutions
- to generate a competitive advantage over competitors
- to increase the company value

Sharing is central to the Forth Industrial Revolution:

"The exchange of 3D objects designs online additionally raises the broader question of how intellectual property (IP) may be controlled as the 3D Printing Revolution takes hold. Undoubtedly 3D Printing is a unique technology in terms of the range of IP variants that it may one day be able to infringe. But whereas illegal copy of a music track only infringes copyright, an elicit 3D print may potentially infringe not just a copyright, but also the design rights in an entire product, patents relating

---

[23] Schwab K, The Fourth industrial Revolution, Portfolio Penguin, 2016

to key parts of its design, and any trademarks (such as product logos) included in the print. Due to 3D printing and 3D scanning, protecting IP in physical things is in the longer term potentially going to prove increasingly difficult"[24]

Hybrid Manufacturing: about 3 decades ago, when robots took place in factories, people predicted that within 10 years all factories would be filled with robots, substituting all human operators. Today, people are still present in factories. In a similar way, people are predicting that additive manufacturing will replace all machining processes. Again, probably it will not. Despite, the future factory *"will be a system of hybrid systems of robots and humans, additive and subtractive manufacturing composites and metals, digital and analog processes, cyber and physical systems, nano and macro scales, and so on. Robots will not completely replace humans, just as additive will not completely replace subtractive manufacturing. Rather, they will work collaboratively with a balanced distribution of responsibility"*[25]

Work Environment: all kind of smart devices such as pads, wearables, or phones will provide the worker with the exact information they need in real time or in a certain situation to perform their task efficiently. Integrated into the digital world

---

[24] Barnatt C, A Brief Guide to Cloud Computing: An essential guide to the next computing revolution. (Brief Histories) Little, Brown Book Group. Kindle Edition, 2010

[25] Wang B, The Future of Manufacturing: a new perspective, Engineering Volume 4, Issue 5, October 2018, Pages 722-728

of the factory, the workers are able to control and monitor production processes through the analysis of data and information supported with these devices. Intelligent assistance systems with optimized. HMI will further make it possible for the worker to make qualified decisions in a shorter time despite the very complex situation on the shop floor.[26]

Work Organization: workers, capable of working and manage digital tools and smart device, will improve the possibilities of job rotation and job enrichment. Moreover, they will act more as controller rather than operators, increasing responsibilities and decision-making power. In this sense, the organization and structure of companies will become flatter. This change will also affect engineers and middle-management as they need to cede part of their decision-making power.[27]

Smart Product Development: the increasing demand for high complexity and new technological developments potentiated by the Fourth Industrial Revolution have led to the development of more complex and smarter products with new capabilities. Smart products integrated with smart production, smart logistics and smart networks will result in the transformation of current value chains and the emergence of new and innovative business models, making the smart factory and smart products key elements of future smart infrastructures. Product development trends are highly

---

[26,26] Gehrke L. et al, A Discussion of Qualifications and Skills in the Factory of the Future: A German and American Perspective, VDI and ASME, April 2015

influenced by new technologies that led to new innovative type of products. Therefore, New Product Development is shifting to Smart Product Development by using new 4.0 technologies such as:

- **Additive Manufacturing**. Benefits include:
    - Rapid prototyping: AM provides a cheap and fast solution to make prototypes. Prototypes are useful in different stages of Product Development, from design concept generation to buy off final products;
    - Tooling & Fixturing: making fixtures, support or masks to support the production process may involve several weeks, from design to manufacturing and shipping. With AM, once the 3D model is ready, the printing process may take hours, maybe days, depending of the size and accuracy. In any case, AM may reduce the lead time from weeks or months to hours or days. In any case, it provides more time to the design phase the most value-added step.
- **Augmented Reality**: at different stages of product development, AR may support the developer in decision making by creating a unique experience at lower cost. Different design solutions and modifications, for example, may be experienced on existing products.
- **Virtual Reality**: similar to AR, VR may support the decision-making process by creating virtual experiences. Moreover, the learning curve can be shortened by using VR as a training tool.

- **Internet of Things, Big Data and Artificial Intelligence**: data collection and analysis with the support of AI provide huge benefits throughout the entire product development lifecycle:
    - Market research: data support the decision-making process to identify the best market segment or the product category it is worth to invest
    - Design concept: data help designers and product development to learn from previous products to improve performances
    - Manufacturing and Assembly processes: data support manufacturing engineers to learn from the past and improve processes
    - Maintenance and Service: smart products are able to share data to predict and prevent failures and catastrophic events
- **Simulation**: Throughout Simulations, engineers are able to identify in advance issues on product design and manufacturing processes and business goals (e.g. throughput per year, scraps, HS&E issues and so on). Discrete Event Simulations and Process Simulation are common tools to support such risk assessments
- **Cloud Computing**: Cloud computing supports virtual teams by sharing information throughout IT tools like data sharing platforms or web conferences. In this way, different skills and capabilities from people located all around the world can be exploited.

Better and faster decision making: it has become crucial to take the right decision at the right time and fast. Wrong decisions may lead to bad products or services and therefore to failure. But good decisions are normally led by intensive use of data and analyses, which are time consuming. Industry 4.0 is based on a massive sharing of data in real time, coming from different sources through cyber physical systems from all different stages of a product life-cycle, from market research, design concept, production, service, maintenance and disposal. Big Data Analytics (this is the "official" term in the Industry 4.0 framework) and Artificial Intelligence (AI) will drive better and faster decision making and shorter time to market.

Better, faster and cheaper products: every consumer is looking for better and reasonably cheaper products, with a shorter time to market. Most of the benefits of Industry 4.0 are of course in product development and production environment. Interconnected machines and new digital technologies make the process flexible, fast and robust.

Higher transparency: the trend of digitalization is currently toward more transparency, meaning more data in the supply chain and more data at the fingertips of consumers and therefore more peer-to-peer comparisons on the performance of products that shift power to end consumers.

QUIZ PART 1

Test your knowledge! Here you will find a series of questions that will help you to revise some basic concepts in Part 1. You will find the correct answers at the bottom of page 61.

1) What is the 4° Industrial Revolution?

1. An industrial trend made of a set of technologies, mainly digital, which aims to revolutionize digital products
2. An industrial trend made of a set of technologies, mainly digital, which aims to improve the performance of future factories, including productivity and product variation
3. A set of brand-new technologies which aims to modernize old factories to reduce production cost and increase competitiveness
4. All of them

2) When and where did Industry 4.0 come to the public?

1. Hannover Fair, November 2011
2. Hannover Fair, November 2015
3. Berlin Fair, November 2011
4. Berlin Fair, November 2015

3) What are the 5 stages of production? Put them in the right order:

1. High volume standardization
2. Low volume standardization
3. High volume customization
4. Mass personalization
5. Low volume customization

4) What are other reasons to implement Industry 4.0?

1. Better, faster and cheaper products
2. Better and faster decision making
3. Better transparency
4. Higher volume
5. Increase profitability

5) What are the 9 key technologies of I4.0 according the BCG?

1. Additive Manufacturing
2. Computer Science
3. Autonomous Robots
4. Cloud computing
5. Cybersecurity
6. Process Engineering
7. Simulation
8. Horizontal and Vertical System Integration

9. Mechatronics
10. Robotics
11. Big Data Analytics
12. Material engineering
13. Software Development
14. Augmented and Virtual Reality
15. Internet of Things

6) Why is Cyber-security critical?

1. Cybercrime is now the fastest-growing industry on the planet
2. Because hackers are becoming smarter
3. The increased interconnectivity of digital devices makes systems more vulnerable to cyber-attack
4. All of them

7) What are some of the ways in which Industry 4.0 is affecting the market?

1. Skills in demand are changing
2. New operating models are being transformed into new digital models
3. Customer expectations are changing
4. Data is becoming a valuable asset
5. New forms of collaboration
6. All of them

8) What are Reconfigurable Manufacturing Systems?

1. RMS are attractive options to handle mass personalization, as the system can be continuously reconfigured in accordance with the demanded volumes and products
2. RMS are attractive options which enable assets to easily move within the factory to change the factory layout with the main goal do adapt to different scenarios
3. RMS are attractive IT systems to reconfigure quickly manufacturing processes by changing machining set up

9) What is the main impact of Industry 4.0 on developing economies?

1. Industry 4.0 will lower the production cost in high wage countries, therefore making the offshoring in developing countries to reduce labor cost not convenient anymore
2. Developing economies need to invest in Industry 4.0 technologies to be competitive with high wage countries, as the labor cost will not be a competitive advantage anymore
3. Developing economies will benefits from Industry 4.0 technologies as the production cost will increase due

to the massive investment requirement, therefore making the low labor cost even more competitive

10) What is the impact of Industry 4.0 on education?

1. Education will massively benefit from the Cloud, as knowledge will become more affordable and accessible
2. Industry 4.0 will increase learning offers, making education more flexible
3. Industry 4.0 will be detrimental for Education, as content quality will be reduced

11) Do you think that Industry 4.0 will create or cut jobs?

12) Which technologies will impact the most in your organization?

13) Do you think that Industry 4.0 is more an opportunity or a threat? Or both?

Correct answers:

1) 2   2) 1   3) 5, 2, 1, 3, 4   4) 1, 2, 3, 5   5) 1, 3, 4, 5, 7, 8, 11, 14, 15   6) 4   7) 10   8) 1   9) 1, 2   10) 1, 2

PART 2: THE KEY TECHNOLOGIES

In the previous chapter, the 9 key technologies have been quickly presented.

In this section, we are going to describe in detail each technology and its main application in the industry.

Below you will find a list of the chapters in Part 2:

Chapter 3: Autonomous Robots... **67**

Chapter 4: Additive Manufacturing..................................... **88**

Chapter 5: Internet of Things (IoT)....................................**120**

Chapter 6: Augmented Reality..**136**

Chapter 7: Virtual Reality **148**

Chapter 8: Big Data Analytics..**160**

Chapter 9: The Cloud **178**

Chapter 10: Simulation **198**

Chapter 11: Horizontal & Vertical IT Systems Integration ..**210**

Chapter 12: Cyber-security...**220**

Chapter 13: Other Technologies **234**

Chapter 3: Autonomous Robots

3.1 Automated Guided Vehicles **68**

3.2 Collaborative Robots (Cobots) **74**

3.3 Drones **82**

Chapter Summary

Robots are the result of the third industrial revolution. The term comes from a Czech word, "robota", meaning "forced labor"; the word 'robot' was first used to denote a fictional humanoid in a 1920 play R.U.R. (Rossumovi Univerzální Roboti – Rossum's Universal Robots) by the Czech writer, Karel Čapek but it was Karel's brother Josef Čapek who was the word's true inventor.

Industrial robots are becoming a key technology in smart factories not only because of their increasing capability and flexibility, but also because they are becoming constantly cheaper (see Figure 8). In this chapter, 3 categories of robots are described: Automated Guided Vehicles, Collaborative Robots and Drones.

Keywords: Robots, Automated Guided Vehicles, AGV, Collaborative Robots, Cobots, Drones

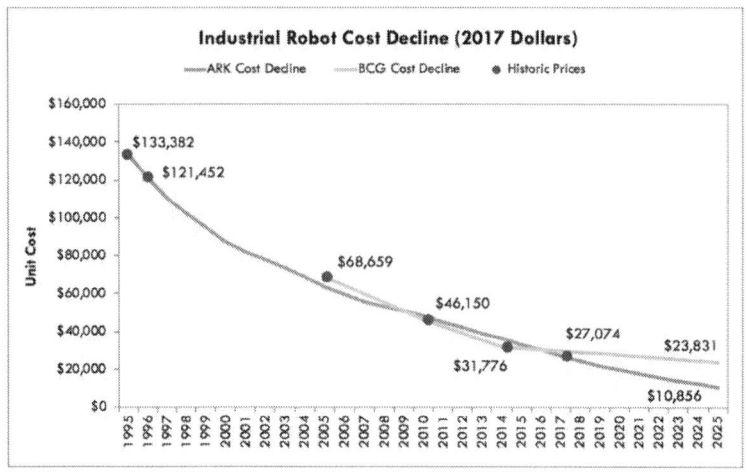

Figure 8: Industrial robot cost decline[28]

3.1 Automated Guided Vehicles

An Automated Guided Vehicle (AGV) is a portable robot that follows markers or wires in the floor, or uses vision, magnets, or lasers for navigation. They are most often used in industrial applications to move materials around a manufacturing facility or warehouse. Applications of the automatic guided vehicle broadened during the late 20th century.

---

28 https://ark-invest.com/articles/analyst-research/industrial-robot-cost-declines/

The first AGV was brought to market in the 1950s, by Barrett Electronics of Northbrook, Illinois, and at the time it was simply a tow truck that followed a wire in the floor instead of a rail. Out of this technology came a new type of AGV, which follows invisible UV markers on the floor instead of being towed by a chain. The first such system was deployed at the Willis Tower (formerly Sears Tower) in Chicago, Illinois to deliver mail throughout its offices.

Automated Guided Vehicles can be used in a wide range of applications and they excel in applications with the following features:

- repetitive movement of materials over a distance
- balanced processes
- regular delivery of stable loads
- processes where tracking material is important

3.1.1. Navigation

The simplest AGVs are based on **wired navigation**, where a slot is cut along the path the AGV has to follow. This wire is used to transmit a radio signal. This solution is quite invasive and not flexible. Better solutions are nowadays available on the market:

- **Guide tape:** the tapes can be one of two styles: magnetic or colored. The AGV is fitted with the appropriate guide sensor to follow the path of the tape. One major advantage of tape over wired guidance is that it can be easily removed and relocated if the course needs to change. Colored tape is initially less expensive, but lacks the advantage of being embedded in high traffic areas where the tape may become damaged or dirty.

- **Laser target navigation:** the navigation is done by mounting reflective tape on walls, poles or fixed machines. The AGV carries a laser transmitter and receiver on a rotating turret. The laser is transmitted and received by the same sensor. The angle and (sometimes) distance to any reflectors that in line of sight and in range are automatically calculated. This information is compared to the map of the reflector layout stored in the AGV's memory. This allows the navigation system to triangulate the current position of the AGV. The current position is compared to the path programmed in to the reflector layout map. The steering is adjusted accordingly to keep the AGV on track. It can then navigate to a desired target using the constantly updating position.

- **Inertial navigation:** another form of an AGV guidance is inertial navigation system (INS). An inertial navigation system is a navigation aid that uses a computer, motion sensors (accelerometers), rotation sensors (gyroscopes), and occasionally magnetic sensors (magnetometers) to continuously calculate by dead reckoning the position, the orientation, and the velocity (direction and speed of movement) of a moving object without the need for external references. It is used on vehicles such as ships, aircraft, submarines, guided missiles, and spacecraft. Other terms used to refer to inertial navigation systems or closely related devices include inertial guidance system, inertial instrument, inertial measurement unit (IMU) and many other variations.

- **Natural feature navigation**: navigation without retrofitting of the workspace is called Natural Features Navigation. One method uses one or more range-finding sensors, such as a laser range-finder, as well as gyroscopes or inertial measurement units with Monte-Carlo/Markov localization techniques to understand where it is as it dynamically plans the shortest permitted path to its goal. The advantage of such systems is that they are highly flexible for on-demand delivery to any location. They can handle failure without bringing down the entire manufacturing operation, since AGVs can plan paths around the failed device. They also are quick to install, with less down-time for the factory.

- **Vision guidance**: Vision-Guided AGVs can be installed with no modifications to the environment or infrastructure. They operate by using cameras to record features along the route, allowing the AGV to replay the route by using the recorded features to navigate. Vision-Guided AGVs use Evidence Grid technology, an application of probabilistic volumetric sensing, and was invented and initially developed by Dr. Hans Moravec at Carnegie

Mellon University. The Evidence Grid technology uses probabilities of occupancy for each point in space to compensate for the uncertainty in the performance of sensors and in the environment. The primary navigation sensors are specially designed stereo cameras. The vision-guided AGV uses 360-degree images and build a 3D map, which allows to follow a trained route without human assistance or the addition of special features, landmarks or positioning systems.

- **Geoguidance:** A geoguided AGV recognizes its environment to establish its location. Without any infrastructure, the forklift equipped with geoguidance technology detects and identifies columns, racks and walls within the warehouse. Using these fixed references, it can position itself, in real time and determine its route. There are no limitations on distances to cover number of pick-up or drop-off locations. Routes are infinitely modifiable.

3.1.2 Path decision

Considering wireless AGVs, paths are pre-programmed. The AGV uses the measurements taken from the sensors and compares them to values given to them by programmers. When it approaches a decision point, it only has to decide whether to follow path 1, 2, 3, etc. This decision is rather simple since it already knows its path from its programming. This method can increase the cost of an AGV because it is required to have a team of programmers to program the AGV with the correct paths and change the paths when necessary.

3.1.3 Traffic control

Flexible manufacturing systems containing more than one AGV may require to have traffic control so the AGV's will not run into one another. Traffic control can be carried out locally or by software running on a fixed computer elsewhere in the facility. Local methods include zone control, forward sensing control, and combination control. Each method has its advantages and disadvantages.

3.1.4 Benefits & Limitations

Cost saving: cost saving comes from implementing automated guided vehicles is a reduction in labor costs because you are either replacing an existing employee or foregoing a new hire.

Safety: they can perform tasks that are dangerous to human workers, such as handling hazardous substances, working in extreme temperatures, and moving heavy materials.

Productivity: AGVs are able to operate 24/7 and in conditions that humans cannot effectively work, which ultimately increases productivity and the bottom line.

Track Inventory: when linked with a warehouse control system or a warehouse management system like Kanban, AGVs easily and automatically track inventory. It means that you know exactly how much material you have, allowing you to order materials when you need them.

Limitations: higher initial investment is a factor to be considered. Moreover, any change takes time and special skills for programming

3.2 Collaborative Robots (Cobots)

A cobot is a robot intended to physically interact with humans in a shared workspace. This is in contrast with other robots, designed to operate autonomously or with limited guidance, which is what most industrial robots were up until the decade of the 2010s.

Cobots are built with safety features such as integrated sensors, passive compliance, or overcurrent detection. The integrated sensors will feel external forces and, if this force is too high, lead the robot to stop its movement. Passive compliance is produced by mechanical components. If an external force acts on a joint, this joint will submit itself to this force. So, in the case of a collision, the joint will move in the opposite direction or stop completely to avoid causing injury.

The term "collaborative robot" is often a misnomer. In fact, although a collaborative robot is designed to work alongside humans, the device itself is not necessarily force limited. This means that the robotic cell is monitored, is safe for human co-workers, and relies on at least one of the 4 collaborative modes.

3.2.1 Collaborative modes

Safety monitored stop: if the human enters the restricted area in the pre-determined safety zone, the robot will stop all movement altogether. Notice that the robot is not shut down, but the brakes are on. An example is provided by FANUC's Dual Check Safety (DCS) control architecture. Dual Check Safety software functions (Position Check, Safe Zones, Safety Speed Check, and Cartesian Position Check) provide safety rated tools for the operator to create safety boundaries to ensure the robot doesn't move outside of restricted spaces.

Hand guiding: this type of collaboration uses regular industrial robots, but with an additional device that 'feels' the forces that the worker is applying on the robot tool. Hand Guidance allows the operator to safely control and guide the robot arm and tooling. In the past, robot movement was usually directed using the teach pendant.

Speed and separation monitoring: the environment of the robot is monitored by lasers or a vision system that tracks the position of the workers. The systems track the position of workers and adapts its speed accordingly.

Power and force limiting: this is the type of robot that everybody calls a collaborative robot. So yes, this is probably the most worker friendly robot since it can work alongside humans without any additional safety devices. They have built-in force torque sensors that detect impact and abnormal forces. The sensors stop the robot when overloaded. This means that if the robot's arm hits something (...like a worker), it automatically stops to protect its human colleagues. These features aren't present on industrial robots, and they're the reason why force limited robots can work alongside humans without any fencing. Regular industrial robots must be isolated because they neither feel nor monitor their environment.

3.2.2 Main Cobots on the market[29]

ABB IRB 1400 Yumi: this robot is specially designed to assemble small electronic devices, so it has the best repeatability out of all the collaborative robots. But there's a potential tradeoff here: with a small payload of just 0.5 kg per arm, electronic boards are basically the only thing it can handle.

---

[29] https://blog.robotiq.com/collaborative-robot-ebook

Features	Values
Degrees of freedom	7 per arm
Payload	0.5 kg per arm
Weight	38 kg
Repeatability	+/- 0.02 mm
Reach	500 mm
Safety	PL b Vat B
Price	40000 USD
Ease of programming	8/10

Table 1: ABB IRB 1400 Yumi Data Sheet

Comau Aura: at a 110 kg payload, the AURA is the cobot with the biggest payload out there. Not only does the robot have a safety skin; it has proximity and tactile sensors embedded in its skin so it can prevent impact and retract depending on the intensity of the impact.

Features	Values
Degrees of freedom	6 per arm
Payload	110 Kg
Weight	685 kg
Repeatability	+/- 0.07 mm
Reach	2210 mm
Safety	proximity and tactile sensors
Price	80000 USD
Ease of programming	6/10

Table 2: Comau Aura Data Sheet

Fanuc CR 35iA: The CR 35iA is one of the biggest collaborative robots on the market and it has a 35 kg payload. It's built over a traditional industrial robot, but its safety features make it safer than any other big robot out there.

Features	Values
Degrees of freedom	6 per arm
Payload	35 Kg
Weight	990 kg
Repeatability	+/- 0.08 mm
Reach	1813 mm
Safety	soft external skin, force torque sensor at the base of the robot: PL d Cat 3
Price	87000 USD
Ease of programming	8/10

Table 3: Fanuc CE 35iA Data Sheet

Kuka LBR IIWA 14 R820: With an excellent power to weight ratio, the LBR IIWA are equipped with highly sensitive force torque sensors at each joint. As opposed to other force limited robots that read the current in their motor, the LBR has sensors that detect micro impacts.

Features	Values
Degrees of freedom	7
Payload	14 Kg
Weight	30 kg
Repeatability	+/- 0.15 mm
Reach	820 mm
Safety	Uses Safe Operation software, Complying to ISO 10218; ISO 12100; ISO 13849
Price	70000 USD
Ease of programming	9/10

Table 4: Kuka LBR IIWA 14 R820 Data Sheet

Universal Robots UR3/U5: The UR3 is designed for polish, glue and screw applications and can be mounted on to a table station for pick-and-place or assembly in optimized production flows. The UR5 stands a bit taller, with a reach radius of 33.5 in (850 mm) and can carry payloads of up to 11 lbs (5 kg). The UR5 is best suited for pick-and-place and testing. The UR10, the largest robot of the trio, is twice as strong as the UR5, with a payload capacity of 22 lbs (10 kg).

Features	UR 3	UR 5
Degrees of freedom	6	6
Payload	3 Kg	5 Kg
Weight	11 kg	18.4 kg
Repeatability	+/- 0.1 mm	+/- 0.1 mm
Reach	500 mm	850 mm
Safety	TUV approved	TUV approved
Price	28000 USD	35000 USD
Ease of programming	8/10	8/10

Table 5: Universal Robots UR3 / U5 Data Sheets

3.2.3 Final considerations on cobots

As already mentioned, the most commonly known "cobots" apply Power and Force Limiting collaborative modes. However, they have some limitations if compared to standard robots:

- they can be significantly more expensive
- they have limited payload capacity

On the other hand, other collaborative modes are probably more recommended for the following reasons:

- standard and less expensive robots are used

- existing robots can be transformed in cobots just by adding additional features like safety stop, limiting and separating speed monitoring functions and hand guiding hardware.

3.3 Drones

Figure 9: A drone[30]

The last category of autonomous robots worth mentioning is commonly known as drone. The term "drone" refers to an

---

[30] https://commons.wikimedia.org/wiki/File:Drone_First_Test_Flight.jpg

unmanned aerial vehicle (UAV), i.e. an aircraft without a human pilot on board. The term unmanned aircraft system (UAS) was adopted by the United States Department of Defense (DoD) and the United States Federal Aviation Administration in 2005 according to their Unmanned Aircraft System Roadmap 2005–2030[31]. In this section, we will use "drone" as main terminology.

Although drones have been developed for military scenarios, in recent years we assisted to an explosion of drones for the civilian market, which is dominated by Chinese companies. Chinese drone manufacturer DJI alone had 74% of civilian-market share in 2018, with no other company accounting for more than 5%, and with $11 billion forecast global sales in 2020[32].

Drones can have different designs, however the most common one is the quadcopter, i.e. a helicopter with four rotors. Quadcopters generally have two rotors spinning clockwise (CW) and two counterclockwise (CCW). Flight control is provided by independent variation of the speed and hence lift and torque of each rotor. Pitch and roll are controlled by varying the net centre of thrust, with yaw controlled by varying the net torque. The four-rotor design allows quadcopters to be relatively simple in design yet highly reliable and maneuverable. Research is continuing to increase

---

[31] "Unmanned Aircraft Systems Roadmap" (PDF). Archived from the original (PDF) on 2 October 2008.

[32] Bateman, Joshua (1 September 2017). "China drone maker DJI: Alone atop the unmanned skies". News Ledge.

the abilities of quadcopters by making advances in multi-craft communication, environment exploration, and maneuverability. If these developing qualities can be combined, quadcopters would be capable of advanced autonomous missions that are currently not possible with other vehicles. For small drones, quadcopters are cheaper and more durable than conventional helicopters due to their mechanical simplicity.[33]

3.3.1 Drones and Industry 4.0

In the context of Industry 4.0, drones have very similar functions as AGVs described in section 3.1, with the main obvious difference that drones fly instead of following paths on the ground. Like AGVs, drones have the capability to move components (lighter) from point A to point B, autonomously or not. Which means, a drone

- can be remotely controlled
- can be programmed to follow a specific path, or
- can fly with a high level of autonomy

Some applications of drones, especially in an industrial context, can be summarized as follows:

- **remote sensing**: drones can carry sensing equipment to assist with any number of functions. Geological surveying, agriculture, archeology, and several other

---

[33] https://en.wikipedia.org/wiki/Quadcopter

industries can benefit greatly from the myriad of sensors that can be packed into a drone. For example, drones can be used in factories to monitor the health of the facility, checking the status of the roof, cranes, ducts and identifying the cause of leaking without using more expensive solutions

- **security & surveillance**: drones can be used to oversee specific areas. Can be used by Police & Security agents in a company
- **disaster relief**: the milieu of sensors that can be packed into a drone can be used to help locate and save life in the midst of natural disasters. Drones can be used to gather and deliver medical samples, supplies, and medicine to remote or otherwise unreachable areas in a disaster zone
- **locating system**: Audi is using a specially developed drone system to locate vehicles that are ready for dispatch at the Neckarsulm site. The flying device flies over the vehicle dispatch area at the Audi site in Neckarsulm autonomously. The drone uses GPS and RFID technology to identify and save the exact position of all vehicles it flew over, thereby helping Audi employees to plan the necessary steps from completion of the vehicles to dispatch to the customers[34]

---

[34]https://www.audi-mediacenter.com/en/press-releases/audi-uses-drones-to-locate-vehicles-at-neckarsulm-site-12999#:~:text=The%20specially%20developed%20hexacopter%2C%20a,of%20the%20cars%20parked%20there.

- **dispatching parts**: in a video showing the smart factory concept by Audi again, you can see how drones can be used to dispatch car components (e.g. a steering wheel) inside the assembly line[35]

---

[35] https://www.youtube.com/watch?app=desktop&v=otE6CnFUXDA

Chapter 4: Additive Manufacturing

4.1 Brief History 89
4.2 Processes and materials 92
4.3 Hybrid manufacturing processes 108
4.4 Design for Additive Manufacturing 109
4.5 Benefits & Challenges 111
4.6 Applications 114

Chapter Summary

Additive Manufacturing is any of various processes in which a material is joined or solidified under computer control to create a three-dimensional object, with material being added together (such as liquid molecules or powder grains being fused together). Other names to indicate this technology are Additive Layer Manufacturing or 3D Printing. Objects can be generated of almost any shape and are produced using digital model data.

In this chapter, a brief history of additive technologies will be provided and the different additive manufacturing processes, as well as the materials used, will be described. Moreover, I will present the main benefits, challenges and applications of 3D printing in various industrial and non-industrial contexts.

Keywords: additive manufacturing, 3D printing, Fused Deposition Modeling, Photopolymerization, Binder Jetting, Material Jetting, Powder Bed Fusion, Laser Sintering, Electron Beam Melting, Design for Additive

4.1 Brief History

- **1981**: Hideo Kodama of Nagoya Municipal Industrial Research Institute published his account of a functional rapid-prototyping system using photopolymers. A solid, printed model was built up in layers, each of which corresponded to a cross-sectional slice in the model.

- **1984**: On 16 July 1984, Alain Le Méhauté, Olivier de Witte, and Jean Claude André filed their patent for the stereolithography process. The application of the French inventors was abandoned by the French General Electric Company (now Alcatel-Alstom) and CILAS (The Laser Consortium). The claimed reason was "for lack of business perspective" Three weeks later, Chuck Hull of 3D Systems Corporation filed his own patent for a stereolithography fabrication system (SLA), in which layers are added by curing photopolymers with ultraviolet light lasers. Hull defined the process as a "system for generating three-dimensional objects by creating a cross-sectional pattern of the object to be formed," Hull's contribution was the STL (Stereolithography) file format and the digital slicing and infill strategies common to many processes today.

- **1988**: The technology used by most 3D printers to date (especially hobbyist and consumer-oriented models) is fused deposition modeling (FDM), a special application of plastic extrusion, developed in 1988 by S. Scott Crump and commercialized by his company Stratasys, which marketed its first FDM machine in 1992.

- **1993**: The term 3D printing originally referred to a powder bed process employing standard and custom inkjet print heads, developed at MIT in 1993 and commercialized by Soligen Technologies, Extrude Hone Corporation, and Z Corporation.

- **1995**: The Fraunhofer Institute developed the Selective Laser Melting process (SLM)

- **2002**: The year of Electron Beam Melting (EBM). Already in 1993, an application was filed by Arcam for a patent describing the principle of melting electrically conductive powder, layer by layer, with an electric beam, for manufacturing three-dimensional bodies. However, 2002 became a turning point in the history of Arcam. With two units installed at clients, the technology was finally ready for commercialization. The first production model, the EBM S12, was launched at EuroMold in Frankfurt at the end of 2002[36]

- **2005**: The RepRap project started in England in 2005 as a University of Bath initiative to develop a low-cost 3D printer that can print most of its own components, but it is now made up of hundreds of collaborators worldwide. RepRap is short for REPlicating RApid Prototyper.

- **2009**: In collaboration with NASA, Contour Crafting techniques are developed. Contour crafting is a building printing technology that uses a computer-controlled crane or gantry to build edifices rapidly and efficiently with substantially less manual labor. Potential applications of this technology include constructing lunar structures of a material that could be built of 90-percent lunar material with only ten percent of the material transported from Earth.

- **2013**: The company Organovo produced a human liver using 3D bioprinting, though it is not suitable for transplantation, and has primarily been used as a medium for drug testing. Organ printing was developed starting from 2003, when

---

[36] http://www.arcam.com/company/about-arcam/history/

Thomas Boland of Clemson University patented the use of inkjet printing for cells. This process utilized a modified spotting system for the deposition of cells into organized 3D matrices placed on a substrate.

4.2 Processes and materials

Most of the material in this section has been collected by the previously mentioned book "3D Printing: Second Edition"[37] by Christopher Barnatt. For those who are interested in a deeper and more extensive understanding on Additive Manufacturing, this book is strongly recommended.

The 7 Additive processes are:

1. Material Extrusion
2. Photopolymerization
3. Material Jetting
4. Binder Jetting
5. Powder Bed Fusion
6. Direct Energy Deposition
7. Sheet Lamination

---

[37] Barnatt C., 3D Printing: Second Edition, CreateSpace Independent Publishing Platform, 2014

4.2.1 Material Extrusion

Material Extrusion refers to any 3D printing process that builds up objects layer-by-layers by putting a semi-liquid material from a computer-controlled nozzle. The most widely extruded materials are thermoplastics that can be temporarily melted for output through a nozzle. The material extrusion of thermoplastics was invented by company Stratasys that labelled the technology 'Fused Deposition Modelling' or 'FDM'. The term FDM has now become commonly used to refer to the extrusion of thermoplastics, and even to material extrusion technologies more generally. Other names for the process are 'Fused Filament Modelling' (FFM), 'Melted and Extruded Modelling' (MEM), 'Fused Filament Fabrication' (FFF) or the 'Fused Deposition Method'.

Figure 10 shows how material extrusion works: a spool of material (the 'filament') is slowly fed to a print head that is heated to between about 180 and 230°C. This high temperature melts the filament, which is then extruded through a fine nozzle. The molten filament is deposited directly onto a flat surface, the 3D printer's 'build platform' or 'print bed'. Here the filament cools and solidifies quickly, with the print head moving to trace out the first layer of the object being printed. Some material extrusion printers move the print head itself on both an upper-down and a right-left axis. Alternatively, others slide the print head back-and-forth on one axis, while moving the build platform on another. This process then repeats and repeats – often over a period of many hours – until a complete object has been printed.

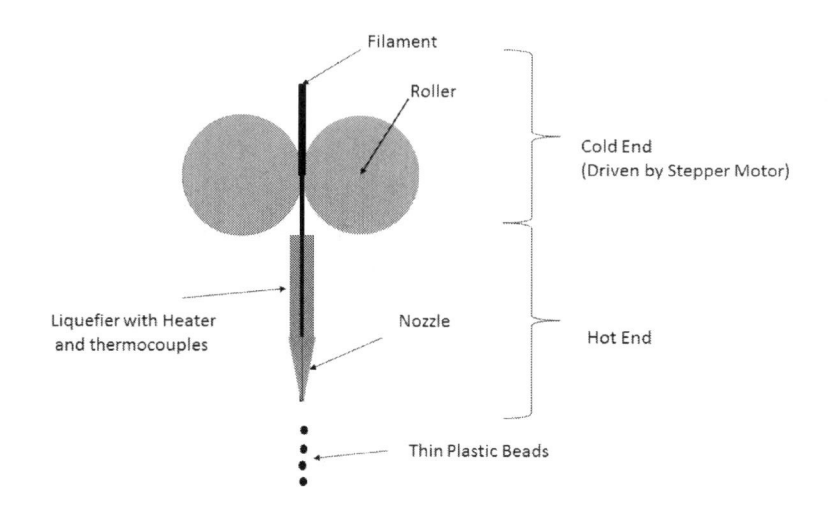

Figure 10: FDM 3D Printer Extruder[38]

Materials

ABS: Acrylonitrile Butadiene Styrene, otherwise known as 'ABS'. This is a petroleum-based thermoplastic that is widely

---

[38] https://commons.wikimedia.org/wiki/File:3D_Printer_Extruder.png

used to injection mold a great many things like Lego bricks, cycle helmets and biros.

PLA: Polylactic Acid, otherwise known as 'PLA'. This is a bioplastic currently made from agricultural produce such as corn starch or sugar cane, and which is subsequently more environmentally friendly than ABS. PLA is also very safe to work with as it does not emit toxic fumes when heated.

Proto-Pasta Carbon Fiber: This is made from PLA compounded 15% by weight with very short-chopped carbon fibers. Proto-Pasta Carbon Fiber printouts are stiffer and resist bending more than standard thermoplastic parts. A similar carbon fiber filament is available from Filabot.

Laywood: Also called Laywoo-D3. Laywood is a composite of sawdust and a polymer binder, and can be melted and then extruded to 3D print objects that feel and smell like wood.

Emerging technologies used with FDM principles are:

WAAM: Researchers at Cranfield University have developed 'wire and arc additive manufacturing' (WAAM). Here a thin titanium wire is threaded through a computer-controlled, movable arm to a print head where it is heated and extruded to build up successive object layers. In December 2013 it was reported that the Cranfield team, working with their industrial partner BAE Systems, had used their WAAM technology to produce a 1.2 m spar section of an aircraft wing. This was 3D printed in titanium in just 37 hours, compared to the many weeks that would have been required for traditional manufacturing methods.

RPD: The Rapid Plasma Deposition™ (RPD™) process was developed by company Norsk Titanium. In RPD, titanium wire is precisely melted in an inert, argon gas environment. The process is monitored more than 600 times per second for quality assurance. Rapid Plasma Deposition™ technology is the ultimate in additive manufacturing. Titanium wire is melted in an inert atmosphere of argon gas and precisely and rapidly built up in layers to a near-net-shape part. The result is significantly less machining, and ultimately, a 50%–75% improvement in buy-to-fly ratio compared with conventional manufacturing methods.

4.2.2 Photopolymerization

"While almost all consumer 3D printers are currently based on material extrusion, many industrial 3D printers use more accurate if more expensive processes that bind powders, solidify liquids, or bond sheets of material together. The first category of these technologies goes under the generic heading of 'vat photopolymerization', and uses a light source to solidify successive object layers on the surface or base of a vat of liquid photopolymer."[39]

---

[39] Barnatt C., 3D Printing: Second Edition, CreateSpace Independent Publishing Platform, 2014

Vat photopolymerization is already commercially achieved via five distinct methods known as
- Stereolithography (SLA)
- Digital Light Projection (DLP)
- Scan, Spin and Selectively Photocure (3SP)
- Lithography-based Ceramic Manufacturing (LCM)
- Two-photon Polymerization (2PP)

For brevity, the most common process, the SLA, is following described.

As previously stated, Stereolithography was the first ever 3D printing process developed by Hideo Kodama, and uses a computer-controlled laser beam to build a 3D object within a vat (or tank) of liquid photopolymer.

Figure 11: How Photopolymerization works shows how Photopolymerization works. In most SLA printer, objects are built on a perforated build platform which is initially positioned just under the surface of a photopolymer vat. A UV laser beam then traces out the shape of the first object layer on the surface of the liquid. This causes it to 'cure' (set solid), then the build platform lowers just a little. More liquid photopolymer then either naturally flows over the top of the first object layer, or is forced across it by a mechanical mechanism, and the next object layer is traced out and set solid by the laser. This process then repeats over and over until the whole object has been printed.

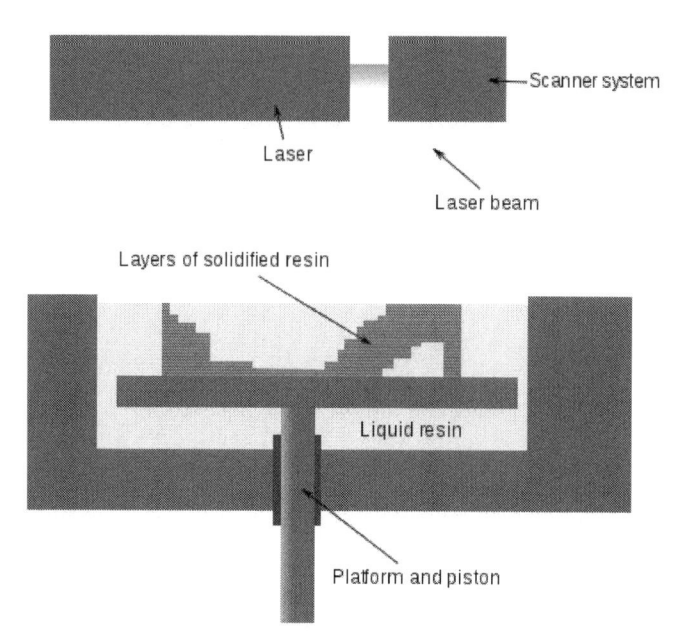

Figure 11: How Photopolymerization works[40]

Materials

Today a wide variety of materials have been developed, including rubber-like plastics, many substitutes for ABS and other thermoplastics, flame retardant plastics, clear resins, and special photopolymers for dental modelling and jewelry design.

---

[40] https://commons.wikimedia.org/wiki/File:Stereolithography_apparatus_vector.svg

Material extrusion VS Photopolymerization

A qualitative comparison between the two main technologies available to consumer is shown in the following table:

Feature	*Material Extrusion*	*Photopolymerization*
Resolution	about 0.1 mm	less than 0.05 mm
Volume	Larger	Smaller
Speed	Slower	Faster
Material cost	Lower	Higher
Material variety	High	Low

Table 6: Material Extrusion VS Photopolymerization

4.2.3 Material jetting

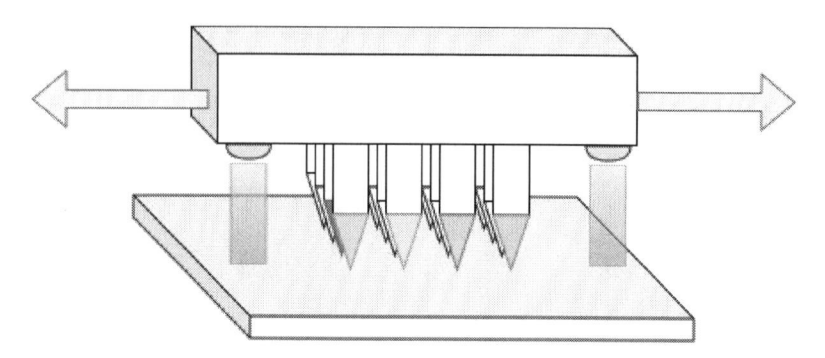

Figure 12: Schematic representation of Inkjet Technology[41]

Material Jetting is another 3D printing technology based on the solidification of liquids.

Material jetting exists in various formats, most of which spray a liquid photopolymer from a multi-nozzle print head. The print head moves across the build platform depositing one layer of liquid photopolymer which is then set solid with UV light also emitted from the print head. 3D printer manufacturer Stratasys sells hardware based on this process under their trademarked name 'PolyJet' (short for 'photopolymer jetting'), while 3D Systems have labelled the technology 'MultiJet Printing' or 'MJP'."

---

[41] https://commons.wikimedia.org/wiki/File:Inkjet_3D_Printing.svg

Materials

A wide range of materials have been created for material jetting, including compounds that simulate the properties of ABS, polypropylene, polycarbonate and rubber. Printers also have the capability to output multiple materials in the same print job by supplying different photopolymers to the print head, and by mixing them in different combinations during the printing process.

4.2.4 Binder jetting

Figure 13: How Binder Jetting works shows how Binder Jetting works. The process starts when a layer of powder is laid on a build platform called the "powder bed". This is usually achieved by raising the base of an adjacent "powder reservoir" and using a sweeper blade to push the powder across the bed. A multi-nozzle print head then travels across the powder bed, selectively jetting a binder solution onto it in the shape of the first object layer. The powder bed is then lowered, another layer of powder is laid down, another layer of binder is jetted onto it, and so on. After the process is completed, a depowdering operation must be processed to remove the powder in excess, typically by compressed air.

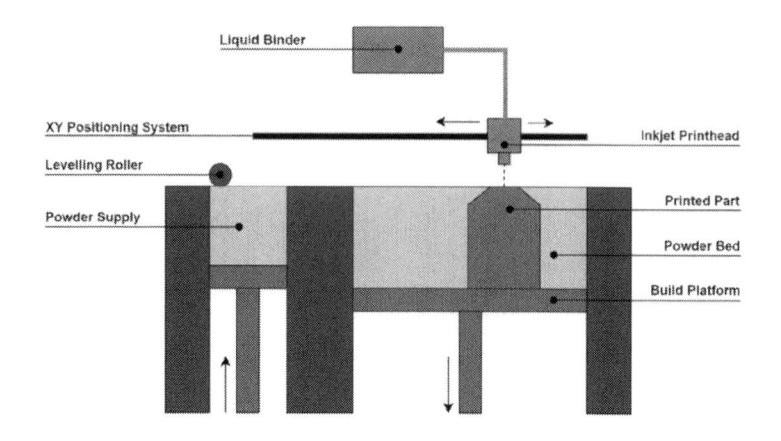

Figure 13: How Binder Jetting works[42]

Benefits of Binder jetting are:

- no support structures have to be printed or removed, as overhangs or orphan parts are always supported by the loose powder that surrounds an object while it is being printed;
- the process is typically faster than other 3D printing methods;
- they are capable of outputting objects in full colour. To make this happen, binder jetting sprays coloured inks as well as binder solution onto each layer of powder. The technology is exactly the same as that used in traditional, 2D photo printers, with cyan, magenta, yellow and black

---

[42] https://commons.m.wikimedia.org/wiki/File:Binder_jetting.png

inks applied in an appropriate combination to produce full colour printouts.

On the other hand, it is not possible to make object 100% solid. To make this happen, it is necessary to turn to Powder Bed Fusion 3D printing technology, which will be described later on.

Materials

Polymer: 3D Systems sells a full-colour binder jetting printer called ProJet 4500 that makes objects from a plastic powder called VisiJet C4 Spectrum. This 3D printer was launched in December 2013 and offers the ability to create semi-rigid plastic parts that require no post-processing.

Sand: some printers can also use casting sand, which allows molds and interior mold sections (the "cores") to be 3D printed, with significant industrial applications. The main benefit of using 3D printing for sand cast molds is that there is no need to create a physical pattern of an object before it is printed (a process that requires time and craft skills). The application of this technology can therefore save a great deal of time and money, as well as allowing novel products to be created.

Metal: bronze, iron or stainless-steel infused with bronze, or nickel-based alloy parts are possible. Parts made by Inconel 625, for example, are used in aerospace to make turbine blades and other high-end industrial components.

Ceramic: the same process used for metals can be used with ceramic materials, such as alumina silica ceramic.

Glass: ExOne has binder jetting hardware to create glass objects.

4.2.5 Powder Bed Fusion

Powder Bed Fusion (PBF) methods use either a laser or electron beam to melt and fuse material powder together. In the following sections we will provide an overview of two of the most common PBF processes: Laser Sintering and Electron Beam Melting.

4.2.5.1 Laser Sintering

In Laser Sintering, also known sometimes as "Laser Beam Melting" (LBM), a layer of powder is rolled (or swept) across a powder bed, following which a laser beam traces out the cross-section of the first object layer. The heat from the laser "sinters" the powder granules that it touches, so causing them to at least partially melt and fuse with adjacent granules.

There are different trademarked variants of laser sintering to use laser beam to fully melt the granules of a single-material powder in order to produce purer metal objects. These processes have some small differences depending on their implementation and the particular manufacturer. Here a list of different laser sintering processes:

- Direct Metal Laser Sintering (DMLS)
- Direct Metal Printing (DMP)
- Selective Laser Melting (SLM)
- Micro-Laser Sintering (MLS)

The surface quality of objects produced via laser sintering is excellent, and a range of finishes can be achieved. The main limitation of laser sintering is the expensive hardware, with each printer typically costing several hundred thousand dollars.

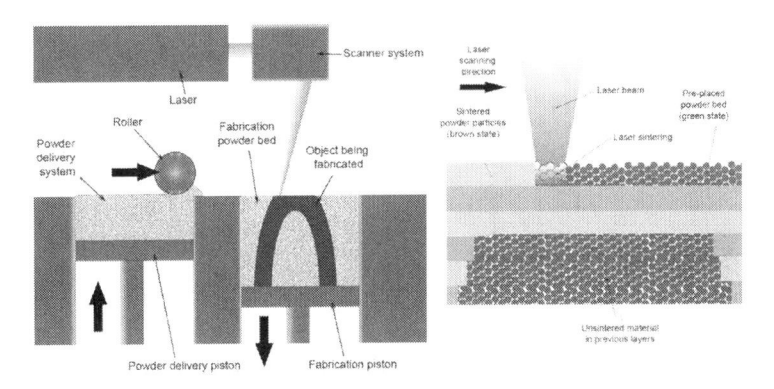

Figure 14: How Laser Sintering works[43]

---

[43] https://commons.wikimedia.org/wiki/File:Selective_laser_melting_system_schematic.jpg

Materials

A wide range of materials can be used, including plastics, many metals, ceramic, sand and wax. Laser sintering is a very accurate process and produces excellent results in plastic materials such as nylon. However, it is not possible to build objects with mechanical properties suitable for some engineering applications like engine components.

4.2.5.2 Electron Beam Melting

Electron Beam Melting (EBM) is also known as Electron Beam Additive Manufacturing (EBAM). The process has been invented by company Arcam, and builds objects layer-by-layer in a vacuum, with electron beam making multiple passes of each object layer. The electron beam moved around via electromagnetic deflection, rather than being directed by mechanically -mechanized mirrors.

The main benefit of EBM over LS is that completely dense metal parts can be accurately created with zero distortion. EBM is used for aerospace and other specialist industrial sectors. Medical implants have also been produced using this technology. The main limitation at the moment is the limited build volume, around 350 x 350 x 380.

4.2.6 Direct Energy Deposition

In Directed Energy Deposition (DED), metal powder is directed into a high-power laser beam for deposition. Unlike in powder bed fusion, the metal powder fed to the print head can be altered continuously during printout. Directed energy deposition can therefore fabricate objects with properties that cannot be obtained using traditional production methods.

Because a flat powder bed is not required, directed energy deposition has the advantage of being able to repair existing objects.

Materials: stainless steel, copper, nickel, cobalt, aluminum and titanium.

4.2.7 Sheet lamination

Sheet Lamination was invented by a company called Helisys in 1991 that has since gone out of business. Sheet lamination refers to a variety of mechanisms, but typically all advance a sheet of build material onto a build platform. This material may have an adhesive backing or have adhesive applied during the process. A laser (or blade) is used to cut the outline of an object layer into the sheet, and the build platform lowers just a little. The process then repeats until all object layers have been created.

Materials

This technology sticks together sheets of paper, plastic or metal foil that are shaped into object layers by cutting them with a laser or blade. Where sheet lamination adheres sheets of paper, it is also known as "laminated object manufacture" (LOM).

4.3 Hybrid manufacturing processes

Hybrid processes refer to the combination of additive and subtractive manufacturing processes applied sequentially or integrated. Several major CNC manufacturers have already introduced bolt-on 3D print heads for their platforms: companies producing new 3D printer systems have likewise begun to incorporate features allowing limited subtractive machining in their processes. The arrival of commonplace "hybrid" manufacturing is probably inevitable, as improvements both in CNC and in 3D printing create larger areas of capability overlap between the two.

Hybrid manufacturing offers a number of benefits over machining or 3D printing alone because of additive's ability to add material just where it is needed. 3D printing also allows for the use of multiple materials in a single part, which makes it possible to clad weaker metals for greater strength, add copper to aid heat transfer or save money on material by applying expensive metals only where they are needed. When additive is combined with machining in a hybrid system, it is possible to 3D print and finish a part in a single setup. This approach reduces error because the printed part does not have to leave the build envelope and be reset on a separate machine. It is also possible to alternate printing and machining to finish internal features, such as conformal cooling channels for injection molds, or features that would be inaccessible in the completed part[44].

Another interesting application of hybrid manufacturing is in repair: for example, if a critical feature is machined below the lower dimensional limit, material can be added via 3D printing and subsequently removed via CNC tools to reach the final dimension.

4.4 Design for Additive Manufacturing

With subtracting machining and standard processes, design is mainly driven by manufacturing processes. Which means, it is not possible to create very complex/ideal geometries for different reasons:

- complex shapes can be simply not feasible

---

[44] https://www.additivemanufacturing.media/articles/am-101-hybrid-manufacturing

- complex shapes are often more expensive

As a relatively new manufacturing technology, engineers and designers have little experience and insufficient knowledge on the capabilities and limitations of AM. Design for Additive Manufacturing (DfAM) have been recently introduced as one of the supplementary design tools for selecting the process parameters (such as cost, time, quality, reliability and CAD constraints) in an optimal manner.

Because "complexity is free", adding complex features and geometries is feasible and doesn't add costs. Topology optimization is a method for obtaining the best possible geometry/shape while satisfying certain requirements. For example, optimization of product's volume while maintaining minimum compliance of parts have frequently investigated. For lower weight-to-stiffness ratio, there exists several novel topology optimization applications.

Another example of a new way of design thinking is Design for Assembly (DfA). In most cases, mechanisms require 2 or more parts to be assembled. Using AM properly, now it is possible to print element and mechanism without any assembly need.

4.5 Benefits & Challenges

Benefits

"I always find it difficult to look at one specific added value that additive manufacturing brings. The fact that you manufacture additively instead of subtractively per definition, in my opinion, always gives you lightweight solutions [...] Lighter weight for me goes hand-in-hand with better stiffness, more complexity, or assembly reduction, so I struggle when I am asked to narrowly focus on a specific added value with this technology. If as a designer I have a new toolbox that can increase the performance of a system five different ways, why would I only focus on one? You can absolutely lightweight parts with additive, but you can do a lot more." Koen Huybrechts, Senior Project Engineer, 3D Systems

Lightweight: nowadays, lightweight is a critical factor in new product design. In fact, lightweight components have several benefits: 1) Lightweight cars or airplanes mean less fuel consumption, which leads to less fuel cost and less pollution; 2) Less material required, which can lead to cheaper components; 3) Buy-to-fly ratio, which means less waste.

Feasibility: with AM, there are almost no design limitations, and components that before were simply impossible to produce, now can be manufactured.

Complexity is free: complex components are traditionally manufactured by casting or milling centers; however, depending on their complexity, costs, set up and processing time may vary significantly. With AM, it doesn't matter how complex a component is, there are no additional cost due to design complexity.

Cost: depending on the method and requirements, parts can be much cheaper than traditional processes. This is particularly true with FDM. For example, Product Development consists of an iterative approach that can involve different design iterations. Each design iteration may imply new tools, fixtures, supports etc. that can be potentially used only few times before the new design iteration. In these scenarios, FDM with polymeric materials may be strong enough and even 80-90% cheaper than traditional items. Another application where AM can result cheaper than traditional processes is Low Volume: indeed, developing a few numbers of items can be extremely expensive as all the development costs should be charged on them.

Rapid prototyping: AM provides a cheap and fast solution to make prototypes. Prototypes are useful in different stages of Product Development, from design concept generation to buy off final products.

Faster: making fixtures, supports or masks to support the production process may involve several weeks, from design to manufacturing and shipping. With AM, once the 3D model is ready, the printing process may take hours, maybe days, depending of the size and accuracy. In any case, AM may reduce the lead time from weeks or months to hours or days.

In any case, it provides more time to the design phase the most value-added step.

Flexibility: AM can print any shape. This means that no additional tooling or fixturing are required, no additional set up or reprogramming.

Personalization: Due to its high flexibility, AM can personalize products. This is particularly useful in fashion businesses, where customers may choose their jewelry depending on their personal taste, or in manufacturing, where selective assembly may be required.

Challenges

Knowledge: The first form of AM was invented in 1981, therefore can't be considered a new technology. However, the knowledge among industries is still quite low, as its potential. AM is considered most of the time a DIY technology for people who want to replicate small plastic objects at home, or, on the other hand, AM is considered something to be used only in high-tech industries. This is definitely a mis-concept: some forms of AM are very cheap and can provide big benefits to Small Middle Enterprises (SME). For final products, although 3D printing components have been already used for high-demanding applications like Formula 1 or aerospace, it is still at quite an early readiness level for mass production applications.

Size: The build volume really depends on the technology to be used, but in general it is not wrong to say that it is quite limited.

Mechanical properties: Although some 3D printed components have been using for high-demanding applications, however in some cases mechanical properties are a limitation.

Cost: Although cost can be cheaper for some application and AM technologies, however it can be extremely high for specific technologies. This can be true when all powder-based technologies are used, as machines and powders are very expensive and the process itself time consuming.

4.6 Applications

Industrial Applications

Rapid prototyping: it is the most popular application. A Replica can be very useful in the following situations:

- show the final product to the customer;
- better evaluation of critical features;
- NC programming to evaluate real space and collisions (e.g. CAM, CMM etc.)
- show features to suppliers for a better understanding

Final products: According to Barnatt, over 20 per cent of 3D printed objects are already end-use components, but by 2020 this figure is expected to rise to at least 50 per cent[45]. In 2016, GE entered a new engine into service called CFM LEAP. This will feature a combustion component that it is not possible to produce using traditional manufacturing methods. Remaining in the aerospace sector, the Boeing 787 Dreamliner has 30 3D printed parts, including air ducts and hinges.

Tools & Fixtures: Typically, manufacturers create tooling in metal as needed by machining it in house or outsourcing it. Depending on the forces experienced by the part, it may not always be necessary to produce these tools in metal. SLA 3D printing materials have advanced significantly, and there are a number of functional resins well suited to 3D printing jigs and fixtures. 3D printed tools and fixtures can be really useful especially in product development. Indeed, plastic materials are nowadays strong enough for a wide range of application, including:

- Fixturing for final inspection (e.g. visual inspection, optical inspection, roughness check, CMM)
- **GO-NOGO gauges**, limited to the tolerances required
- **Support for NDE** (e.g. Magnetic Particle Inspection, Nital Etching, Fluid Particle Inspection, Barkhausen etc.)
- **Small tools for manual operations**, like sealing, gluing and son on;

---

[45] Barnatt C., 3D Printing: Second Edition, CreateSpace Independent Publishing Platform, 2014

- **Machine set up**: calibration jigs as well as machine repair and maintenance tools improve line startup efficiency when getting production up to speed
- **Fixturing and positioning**: soft jaws, assembly jigs, and other work-holding devices require alignment features that can be hard to machine

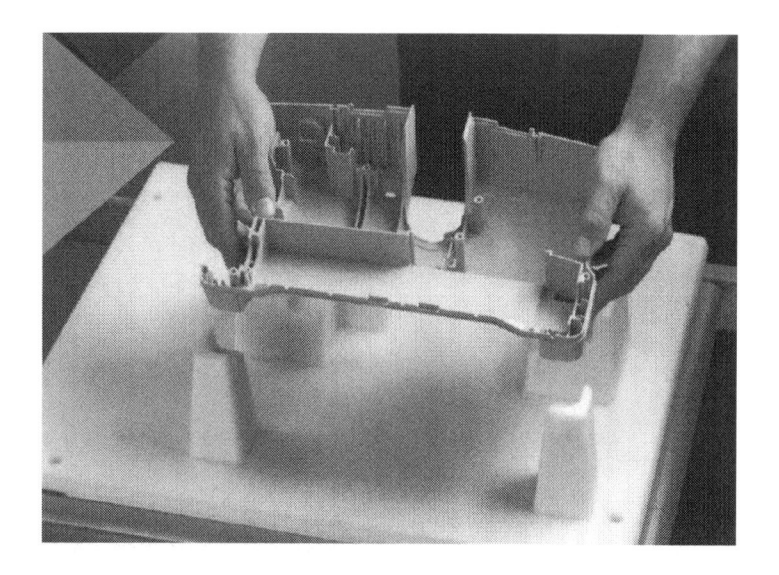

Figure 15: Example of 3D printed support for final inspection[46]

Shadowboards: They are useful to keep the workspace organize and it is part of 5S techniques. Typically produced with foam, shadowboards can be easily produced with 3D

---

[46] Stratasys white paper, 3D PRINTING JIGS & FIXTURES FOR THE PRODUCTION FLOOR

printing techniques as well, especially in conditions of high-cleanliness level requirements

Maintenance: In some situations, machines are stopped because a simple connector, socket, tube is broken and can take days or sometimes even weeks before receiving a spare part. 3D printed items represent a valid temporary solution

Masks and protections: Especially for high-value components, it is important to avoid any scratch or damage during manufacturing steps. For example, in gear industry is it very common to protect critical surfaces with plastic protections. depending on volumes, these can be pretty expensive, as they are typically produced by injection molding, with the mold milled in a milling centres. 3D printed masks and protections can save a significant amount of time and reduce costs. Moreover, similar protections are required in special processes like surface finishing operations. Shot peening, for example, requires rubber mask to protect areas where the treatment is not required.

Molds: in previous section, we have seen how binder jetting can use sand to create sand casting molds. Other materials and technologies can be exploited

Other Applications

3D printed vehicles: 3D printing has already been used to help produce two working automobiles. The first of these is called

"Urbee", created in 2011 by Jim Kor and his company Kor EcoLogic. Urbee is a low-energy, 2-passenger hybrid vehicle[47]. The engine and most interior components are not 3D printed, however Urbee's body shell was built layer-by-layer on Stratasys hardware in 10 thermoplastic sections and took about 2500 hours to print. Another example of 3D vehicle is a bike frame printed by the UK company Renishaw, which has been featured in the 2015 edition of Guinness World Records for manufacturing the world's first 3D printed titanium alloy bicycle frame. The project was completed in collaboration with British bike manufacturer Empire Cycles.

3D printed surgical models: at Kobe University School of Medicine in Japan, Maki Sugimoto is using 3D printers to create medically-accurate models of patient kidneys, livers and other organs, derived from MRI and CT scan data, and can prove invaluable in planning surgery. Model organs are created used material jetting 3D printers that can build things in multiple materials.

3D printed prosthesis: According to a statement made by the American Orthotics and Prosthetics Association, the average prosthetic costs between $1,500 to $8,000. This expense is often paid out of pocket rather than covered by insurance. By contrast, a 3D printed prosthetic costs as little as $50! 3D printed prosthetics can also be made much quicker; a limb can

---

[47] Barnatt C., 3D Printing: Second Edition, CreateSpace Independent Publishing Platform, 2014

be made in a day. Furthermore, consumers can easily customize their purchases, which is another enticing factor for kids. Children can pick out colors and styles to fit their wants and needs.

Bioprinting: The US company Organovo produces a 3D printer called the Novogen MMX that 3D prints layers of living human cells, and is at the forefront of research into organic "bioprinting". The Bioprinting of replacement human tissue is without doubt the most radical application of 3D printing so far conceived. Technically speaking, bioprinting is a bioadditive manufacturing technology and an extension of the science of tissue engineering.

Chapter 5: Internet of Things (IoT)

5.1 Introduction to Internet of Things 121

5.2 Brief History 124

5.3 Industrial Internet of Things (IIoT) 125

5.4 Cyber-Physical Systems (CPS) 126

5.5 Establishing a communication 127

5.6 IoT Protocol & Standards 129

5.7 Applications of IoT 129

Chapter Summary

Internet of Things is probably the most popular concept associated with Industry 4.0. In the first chapter, we have seen that Internet of Things is the primary technology to be exploited, according to Henning Kagermann, Wolf-Dieter Lukas and Wolfgang Wahlster. In this chapter, we will describe Internet of Things in more detail, we will see how IoT enables the development of cyber-physical-systems and we will present what the main challenges are. Finally, practical applications of Industrial Internet of Things (IIoT) will be shown.

Keywords: Internet of Things, IoT, Industrial Internet of Things, IIoT, Cyber-Physical-Systems

5.1 Introduction to Internet of Things

The Internet of things (IoT) is the network of devices that contain electronics, software, actuators, and connectivity which allows these things to connect, interact and exchange data. IoT involves extending Internet connectivity beyond standard devices to any range of traditionally non-internet-enabled devices and everyday objects.

In the article published by the Economist "Siemens and General Electric gear up for the internet of things", it is pointed out that linking the physical and the digital worlds via the IoT could create up to $11 trillion in economic value annually by 2025, estimates the McKinsey Global Institute. A third of that could be in manufacturing[48].

In 2019, Engineering.com conducted a research sponsored by Siemens PLM Software, regarding the importance of IoT in Product Development[49]: 234 product development professionals have ben surveyed about their company's intentions regarding adding IoT functionality to their products. The respondents came from a wide range of industries, representing processed goods, component and part

---

[48] Siemens and General Electric gear up for the internet of things, https://www.economist.com/business/2016/12/03/siemens-and-general-electric-gear-up-for-the-internet-of-things , 3 Dec, 2016

[49] Research Report: The State of IoT Adoption in Product Development 2019, Engineering.com, 2019

manufacturers, and finished goods OEMs. Here are a few highlights:

- IoT functionality in product development became more prevalent
- Respondents who held roles of manager and above generally considered implementing IoT enabled features to be more important than other members of a product development team
- Teams who are evaluating IoT enabled products are exploring a wide range of business models and product features

The importance of interconnected systems can be summarized in 4 concepts:

- data-driven decision making
- communication
- Just in Time
- Adaptability

Data-driven decision making: it means making decisions that are backed up by hard data rather than making decisions that are intuitive or based on observation alone. As business technology has advanced exponentially in recent years, data-driven decision making has become a much more fundamental part of all sorts of industries, including important fields like medicine, transportation and equipment manufacturing.

Communication: the importance of communication between physical assets can be described as follow:

- Data from physical assets promotes motivation by informing and clarifying the employees about the task to be done
- Communication improve the decision-making process, as stated above
- Data assist in controlling processes. Sharing information improve the level of understanding at all company´s level, both in vertical (hierarchic) and horizontal (equal), improving transparency

Just in Time: JIT is a methodology aimed primarily at reducing times within production system as well as response times from suppliers and to customers. Its origin and development were in Japan, largely in the 1960s and 1970s at Toyota. Since within IoT systems communicate and share data in real-time, there is no waste of time between the sending and the receiving of the information. Moreover, IoT implies the use of other 4.0 technologies like AI and autonomous robots so actions can be taken autonomously with almost no additional time required.

Adaptability: the downstream operations are influenced by upstream processes. Therefore, upstream changes mean effectively that downstream processes need to adapt themselves to new operating conditions. Techniques like Six Sigma, for example, aim to produce long-term defect levels below 3.4 defects per million opportunities (DPMO). However, especially in the context of high-personalization production, where products variation is increasingly higher, to achieve this target is simply not cost effective. In this sense, IoT technologies will create a new process paradigm, where flexible and adaptable process will deliver high-quality products with less human effort.

5.2 Brief History

- **1982**: the concept of a network of smart devices was discussed as early as 1982, with a modified Coke machine at Carnegie Mellon University becoming the first Internet-connected appliance able to report its inventory and whether newly loaded drinks were cold.

- **1991**: Mark Weiser's paper on ubiquitous computing, "The Computer of the 21st Century", as well as academic venues such as UbiComp and PerCom produced the contemporary vision of IoT. In 1994, Reza Raji described the concept in as "[moving] small packets of data to a large set of nodes, so as to integrate and automate everything from home appliances to entire factories".

- **1999**: the term "Internet of things" was likely coined by Kevin Ashton of Procter & Gamble, later MIT's Auto-ID Center, though he prefers the phrase "Internet for things". He viewed

Radio-frequency identification (RFID) as essential to the Internet of things.

5.3 Industrial Internet of Things (IIoT)

IIoT is simply the application of IoT to industrial applications, including, but not limited to, manufacturing and energy management. Despite IoT, IIoT history begins earlier, in 1968, with the invention of the programmable logic controller (PLC) by Dick Morley, a General Motors employee. With the introduction of Ethernet in 1980, people began to explore the concept of a network of smart devices, and IoT era then started with the Coke machine, as explained before.

One of the first consequences of implementing the IIoT would be to create instant and ceaseless inventory control. Another benefit of implementing an IIoT system is the ability to create a digital twin of the system. Utilizing this digital twin allows for further optimization of the system by allowing for experimentation with new data from the cloud without having to halt production or sacrifice safety, as the new processes can be refined virtually until they are ready to be implemented. A digital twin can also serve as a training ground for new employees who won't have to worry about real impacts to the live system.

5.4 Cyber-Physical Systems (CPS)

CPS are the essence of IoT and IIoT. Essentially, CPS are physical assets that are able to communicate and share information by using "cyber" technologies.

These cyber-technologies can be grouped as follow:

- **Embedded controllers:** they consist of small computers that allow engineers to add "intelligence" to products at a relatively low cost.
- **Sensors:** a wide range of sensors can be used to monitor systems like accelerometers, gyroscopes, temperature and humidity sensors, pressure sensors, optical sensors and so on.
- **Wireless Technologies:** the most commonly known are Bluetooth, LTE, Wi-Fi.

IoT combines the "brains" of embedded controls, the modularity of smart sensors, and the ubiquitous connectivity of wireless communication.

As a result, the automated manufacturing systems as of today and even more in the future are going to be a composition of software, data, which form a digital twin along with the electronics and mechanical hardware of the physical systems. A full integration of cyber physical systems and availability of a digital twin, i.e. a cyber representation which could be managed in a cyber or physical way, is still a future vision as a number of frontiers of the automation technology as of today need to be overcome.

The following issues have been raised and need attention:

- Improved techniques are required for establishing the communication between the components of the cyber physical systems in order to reduce the effort for interoperability
- New types of standards, e.g. for the semantic processing of information, are required but are difficult to conceive.
- Means to manage the complexity of very large automation systems a yet to be invented.
- The topics of analytics, machine learning and artificial Intelligence need to be deployed to enable Self-X functionalities and present limitation in automatic adjustment of systems.

5.5 Establishing a communication

Different technologies enable wireless communications, the most common are:

- Barcodes, QR codes, Data Matrix etc
- Bluetooth
- Wi-Fi

- GSM, LTE, 4G, 5G etc
- Near Field Communication (NFC)
- Radio-frequency Identification (RFID)

Position tracking can be also considered a way to interconnect systems, as they provide "info" about their position. In this sense, additional technologies are:

- Global Positioning System (GPS), used for outdoor tracking
- Infrared (IR), used for indoor tracking
- Digital Camera

The adoption of the Internet of Things is driven by the falling cost of smart sensors and the ease with which, as they become ever smaller, they can be deployed into new products.

RFID is probably one of the most widely used technology, due to its simplicity and low cost. In 2014, the world RFID market was worth US$8.89 billion, up from US$7.77 billion in 2013 and US$6.96 billion in 2012. This figure includes tags, readers, and software/services for RFID cards, labels, fobs, and all other form factors. The market value is expected to rise to US$18.68 billion by 2026.

5.6 IoT Protocol & Standards

We have already shown how interconnectivity between CPS implies the usage of different technologies (e.g. RFID, GSM, GPS, BLE etc.) each one relying on different protocols and standards. Therefore, it becomes clear how important is to establish the right standard in order that systems can communicate and interact.

Just to make an analogy with human communication, everyone recognizes how useful is to have a common language to speak when we meet people from other countries. This aspect became crucial with globalization. Somehow English has been recognized as a "Lingua Franca", i.e. as "a common means of communication for speakers of different first languages"

With the same logic, it would be useful to have a "Lingua Franca" to enable system to speak the same language.

5.7 Applications of IoT

5.7.1 Industrial Applications

Asset Tracking: it refers to the method of tracking physical assets, either by scanning barcode labels attached to the assets or by using tags using GPS, BLE or RFID which broadcast their location. These technologies can also be used for indoor tracking of persons wearing a tag.

Asset inventory

- Helps to manage physical capitals and allow to make more informed decisions regarding inventory, such as when to repair or replace items;
- Maximizes employee and equipment efficiency;
- Reduces equipment downtime through better planning;
- Prevents theft and enhance security of items.

Flexible / Reconfigurable Manufacturing Systems: Reconfigurable manufacturing systems (RMSs) are attractive options for handling product personalization, as the system can be continuously reconfigured in accordance with the demanded volumes and products. However, the development of the RMS is a particularly challenging task compared to the development of a traditional manufacturing system[50].

---

[50] Bejlegaard M et al, Reconfigurable Manufacturing Potential in Small and Medium Enterprises with Low Volume and High Variety, 3rd International Conference on Ramp-up Management (ICRM), Procedia CIRP 51 (2016), 32–37

Predictive maintenance: Machines are subjected to periodical maintenance to prevent in service failures which can cause a lot of problems in a production system:

- low productivity
- higher cost
- unpredicted repair time, causing longer lead time and in the end lower customer satisfaction

Total Productive Maintenance (TPM) is a Lean technique and it focuses on keeping all equipment in top working condition to avoid breakdowns and delays in manufacturing processes. TPM can be considered a Level II approach (Planned).

Today, the combined benefits of the cloud, including lower cost of ownership, high-power computing resources and IoT connectivity capabilities, have enabled more advanced AI-based systems that leverage machine learning to generate higher-value analytics than more basic, model-based systems. Which means, in other words, that it is now possible to predict breakdowns caused machine failures by monitoring the health of key subsystems, such as spindles, electric motors, bearings and so on.

Statistical Process Control: SPC is a widely used Quality tool in Industry to monitor process deviations. The basic idea is to monitor key process variables (KPV) to prevent defects. This mean that data must be recorded and subsequently analyzed.

IoT enables automatic solution for Data Collection. A typical example are smart gauges which can automatically collect measured values. The same principle is applied on smart torque wrenches which record and collect torque an angle value. Such data can be then automatically analyzed and eventually a real-time feedback (e.g. warning or corrective action) can be provided by AI system.

Mistake proofing: also called Poka-Yoke, mistake (or error) proofing is a technique used by lean manufacturing to prevent mistakes. Some examples are:

- barcode, QR code or RFID instead of human readable methods prevent typos;
- smart torque wrenches use RFIDs to automatically set different torque values for different applications;
- asset tracking can be used to prevent people from taking wrong parts or assemble parts in the wrong position by tracking the arm

5.7.2 Other Applications

Smart home: home automation implies the application of smart technologies in a home environment. Some examples are:

- **Energy control**: it is possible to have remote control of all home energy monitors over the internet incorporating a simple and friendly user interface;
- **Light control system**: a "smart" network that incorporates communication between various lighting system inputs and outputs, using one or more central computing devices;
- **Using Voice control devices** like Amazon Alexa, Google Home or mobile applications to manage coffee machines, ovens, fridge etc.;

Healthcare: medical data can be collected throughout different sensors and devices (e.g. smart bands used for running). Below a couple of interesting applications:

- Alcon (part of Novartis) has licensed Google's smart lens technology which involves non-invasive sensors embedded within contact lenses. The lenses may eventually be able to measure glucose levels of diabetes patients via their tears and then store the information in a mobile device, though Novartis backtracked on a plan to test the system in 2016
- Some dental insurances provide connected toothbrush to offer special deals to their affiliates by monitoring their daily cleaning behavior.

Remote monitoring: big constructions like Dams, Bridges, Buildings, Tunnels and so on can be constantly monitored in real-time.

Shopping: Amazon introduced computer vision and machine learning inside supermarkets, called Amazon GO. You get access through your mobile phone scanning a QR code, then cameras and algorithms create your virtual cart. No final cashier, simply leave the shop and you will be charged automatically.

Chapter 6: Augmented Reality

6.1 Brief History 137
6.2 How AR works 138
6.3 Hardware & Software 140
6.4 Main AR smart glasses available on the market 141
6.5 Main Challenges 143
6.6 Main Applications 145

Chapter Summary

> *"According to the Augmented / Virtual Reality Report 2017 (Digi-Capital, 2017), the VR/AR market should reach $108 billion revenues by 2021, while an overview by Goldman Sachs (2016) suggests a business of $80 billion in 2025"*[51].

In this chapter, we will see how Augmented Reality evolved through the years, how it works, what hardware is required, how to develop the required algorithms and what smart glasses are available on the market: In the past part, we will present some main barriers in using this technology and what the main applications are.

Keywords: Augmented Reality, AR, Smart Glasses

---

[51] Gandolfi E, Handbook of Research on K-12 Online and Blended Learning (2nd ed.), Publisher: ETC Press, Editors: Kennedy, K, Ferdig, R.E., pp.545-561

6.1 Brief History

- **1968**: Ivan Sutherland invented the first VR head-mounted display at Harvard University, called "the Sword of Damocles"

- **1984**: In the movie "The Terminator", the Terminator uses a heads-up display in several parts of the film. In one part, he accesses information about his "new" motorbike

- **1990**: The term 'Augmented Reality' is attributed to Thomas P. Caudell, a former Boeing researcher

- **1994**: Julie Martin creates "Dancing in Cyberspace", the first augmented reality theater production. In "Dancing", acrobats dance in and around virtual objects on stage.

- **1999**: Hirokazu Kato created ARToolKit at HITLab

- **2013**: Google announces an open beta test of its Google Glass augmented reality glasses. The glasses reach the Internet through Bluetooth, which connects to the wireless service on a user's cellphone. The glasses respond when a user speaks, touches the frame or moves the head.

- **2015**: Microsoft announces Windows Holographic and the HoloLens augmented reality headset. The headset utilizes various sensors and a processing unit to blend high definition "holograms" with the real world

- **2017:** IKEA released its augmented reality app called IKEA Place that changed the retail industry forever

6.2 How AR works

Augmented Reality works according to one of the following approaches:

1. **SLAM:** Simultaneous Localization and Mapping (SLAM) is the computational problem of constructing or updating a map of an unknown environment while simultaneously keeping track of an agent's location within it. There are several algorithms known for solving it. Published approaches are employed in self-driving cars, unmanned aerial vehicles, autonomous underwater vehicles, planetary rovers, newer domestic robots and even inside the human body.

2. **Recognition Based:** recognition (or marker) based augmented reality uses a camera to identify visual markers or objects, such as a QR/2D code or natural feature tracking (NFT) markers, to showcase an overlay only when the marker is sensed by the device. Marker-based AR technology depends upon device camera to distinguish a marker from other real-world objects. Not only the marker image but the position and orientation can also be calculated. Once recognized, the marker on screen is replaced with a virtual 3D version of the corresponding object. This is done to permit the user to observe the object in more detail and from various angles. Rotating the marker would rotate the virtual replication as well.[52]

3. **Location Based:** unlike recognition based, location-based AR relies on GPS, digital compass, velocity meter, or accelerometer to provide data about the location and the augmented reality visualizations are activated based on these inputs. It is also known as markerless augmented reality. The location detection features in smartphones make it easy to leverage this type of augmented reality technology, making it quite popular. Some common uses of location-based AR include mapping directions, finding nearby services, and other location-centric mobile apps. A

---

[52] Know the Augmented Reality Technology: How does AR Work? https://www.newgenapps.com/blog/augmented-reality-technology-how-ar-works

popular example is provided by Pokémon Go. The game uses your phone's GPS, camera, and clock to generate a brightly-colored, fantastical version of the real world on your phone[53]. Much like Google Maps, "Pokémon Go" tracks your phone's location using GPS, integrating this information with an in-game map.

6.3 Hardware & Software

Hardware components for augmented reality are:

- processor
- display
- sensors
- input devices

Displays are typically smart glasses, smartphones and tablets. Nowadays, tablets and smartphones are also very common and widely used with AR. These devices have all features required: portable, powerful CPU, digital camera, GPS, inertial sensors and a touch screen. According to Time Magazine, in about 15–20 years it is predicted that Augmented reality and

---

[53,53] Know the Augmented Reality Technology: How does AR Work? https://www.newgenapps.com/blog/augmented-reality-technology-how-ar-works

virtual reality are going to become the primary use for computer interactions[54].

The software must derive real world coordinates from camera images. That process is called image registration, and uses different methods of computer vision. Augmented Reality Markup Language (ARML) is a language specifically developed for AR. To enable rapid development of augmented reality applications, some software development kits (SDKs) have been developed. Some AR SDKs are offered by:

- Vuforia
- ARToolKit
- Catchoom CraftAR Mobinett AR
- Wikitude
- Meta
- ARLab

6.4 Main AR smart glasses available on the market

Google Glass: while it failed to find purchase in the consumer market, Google's foray into Augmented Reality has seen considerably more success in medical and manufacturing applications. The device features some ambitious technology, including bone conduction for audio output and a prism projector display.

The successor to the Explorer Edition, Google Glass Enterprise Edition eschews the bone conduction tech, but also makes several improvements over previous iterations, including an Intel Atom processor and a barometer.

Microsoft HoloLens: billed as the world's first full untethered holographic computer, the HoloLens is available in both a Development Edition and a Commercial Suite configuration. Companies based in North America also have the option of renting a HoloLens through a Microsoft partner. The current version of the HoloLens has a 35° FOV, but a recent patent from Microsoft for a MEMS laser scanner could increase the FOV for the next generation of HoloLens to 70°.

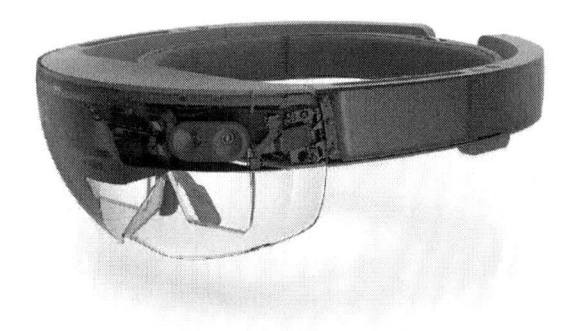

Figure 16: Microsoft HoloLens Headset[55]

---

[55] https://commons.wikimedia.org/wiki/File:Ramahololens.jpg

VUZIX M100 & M300 Smart Glasses: founded in 1997, Vuzix has a long history in the augmented reality industry. Its current offerings suitable for industrial applications are the M100 and M300 Smart Glasses. The M300 is marketed as having enhanced functionality, and there are some important differences between the two. For example, the diagonal FOV on the M100 is 15° and 20° on the M300.

DAQRI Smart Glasses: the latest iteration of the company's augmented reality hardware, DAQRI's Smart Glasses are designed for professional use. The unit is based on a 6th generation Intel Core m7 processor and uses dual LCoS optical displays, which give it a 44° diagonal FOV. It comes equipped with Worksense Standard, DAQRI's suite of apps for AR tasks.

6.5 Main Challenges

User Interface: one of the main challenges of AR is to improve field of view (FOV), brightness, display quality, latency, etc. In the case of FOV, for example, even the best AR HUDs can only offer up to 90 degrees. Compare that to the 190-degree horizontal and 120-degree vertical FOVs for normal human vision and the gap between where the technology is now and where it needs to go becomes obvious.

Health issues: intense use of VR headset might cause some health issues like:

- **Virtual Reality Sickness:** VR headsets contain 2 small LCD monitors, each projected at one eye, creating a stereoscopic effect which gives users the illusion of an artificial environment created all around you. And longer time of screen focus increase feeling of nausea and distortion, a phenomenon called Virtual Reality Sickness
- **Eye Strain:** While using AR/VR headsets we are confined in a limited area from our environment. And we see and focus on particular details for long due to which we may tend to blink less compared to normal frequency of blinking. This results in drying of the front surface of our eyes and strain on eyes
- **Dizziness:** Individuals having amblyopia (an imbalance in visual strength between the 2 eyes) or other conditions inhibits focusing, depth perception or normal 3D vision may not experience 3D effects of VR headsets. Individuals with these disorders may be more likely to experience headaches and eye fatigue when using VR gear

Lack of knowledge: There is still quite a lack of knowledge about this technology and an insufficient level of digitalization within the company

6.6 Main Applications

Facility planning: facility planning is a high risk and high investment process. Layout design is typically performed in 2D or in a 3D CAD environment, which in most case represent a "good enough" approach. On the other hand, other issues like ergonomics can't be easily assessed without expensive simulation software (e.g. Jack by Siemens). AR can help the factory planner to experience how new machines or new production lines fit in the existing space and if workbenches and conveyors have been designed at the right height to avoid ergonomic issues.

Smart drawings: especially for components with complex geometry, AR may help to understand main features of a drawing. AR may help to understand how parts should work in services, highlighting critical features and adding more info like specifications, materials, method of manufacture and method of assembly. Possibilities are limitless.

Learning: similar to smart drawings, AR may increase the learning effectiveness by providing more realistic experiences in the learning process.

Product Development Process: At different stages of product development, AR may support the developer in decision making by creating a unique experience at lower cost. Different design solutions and modifications, for example, may be experienced on existing products.

Quality inspection: AR can support quality inspector during their normal activities. These types of solution are becoming more and more popular.

Assembly instructions: like quality inspection, AR supports workers in the factory to assemble complex components. Instructions like torque values, assembly sequences, tooling to use are displayed to guide the fitter step by step through the entire process

Maintenance Repair and Overhaul (MRO): augmented reality can enhance a worker's ability to perform maintenance routines by superimposing simple step-by-step instructions on their field of view. This is the logical next step in being able to see machine status at a glance using AR, which is a benefit that goes beyond MRO applications.

Plant Maintenance: in a similar way, instructions for maintenance procedures may be provided.

Chapter 7: Virtual Reality

7.1 Brief History 149

7.2 How VR works, hardware and software 152

7.3 Main benefits, limitations and applications of VR 158

Chapter Summary

Virtual Reality (VR) is an interactive computer-generated experience taking place within a simulated environment. It incorporates mainly auditory and visual feedback, but may also allow other types of sensory feedback like haptic. This immersive environment can be similar to the real world or it can be fantastical. In this chapter, we will see how this technology evolved through years, what the two main VR technologies are and how they work. In the final section, we will present some benefits, challenges and real applications in industrial contexts.

Keywords: Virtual Reality, VR, Headset Technology, CAVE

7.1 Brief History

- **1838:** the stereoscope is invented by Sir Charles Wheatstone. This is our first foray into 3D graphics

- **1950:** Morton Heilig's Sensorama. In the mid-1950s cinematographer Morton Heilig developed the Sensorama (patented 1962) which was an arcade-style theatre cabinet that would stimulate all the senses, not just sight and sound. It featured stereo speakers, a stereoscopic 3D display, fans, smell generators and a vibrating chair

- **1960:** the first VR Head Mounted Display. Morton Heilig's next invention was the Telesphere Mask and was the first example of a head-mounted display (HMD)

- **1961:** two Philco Corporation engineers (Comeau & Bryan) developed the first precursor to the HMD as we know it today – the Headsight. It incorporated a video screen for each eye and a magnetic motion tracking system, which was linked to a closed-circuit camera

- **1965:** The Ultimate display by Ivan Sutherland. Ivan Sutherland described the "Ultimate Display" concept that could simulate reality to the point where one could not tell the difference from actual reality. His concept included: 1) a virtual world viewed through an HMD and appeared realistic through augmented 3D sound and tactile feedback; 2) computer hardware to create the virtual world and maintain it in real time; 3) the ability users to interact with objects in the virtual world in a realistic way

- **1968:** The Sword of Damocles is invented by Ivan Sutherland. His invention tracked user head motion and overlayed vision with synthetic computer-generated graphics of primitive 3D object wireframes

- **1987:** Jaron Lanier, founder of the visual programming lab (VPL), coined the term "virtual reality". Jaron developed a range of virtual reality gear including the Dataglove (along with Tom Zimmerman) and the EyePhone head mounted display. They were the first company to sell Virtual Reality goggles (EyePhone 1 $9400; EyePhone HRX $49,000) and gloves ($9000)

- **1991:** Virtuality Group Arcade Machines: The Virtuality Group launched a range of arcade games and machines. Players would wear a set of VR goggles and play on gaming machines with real-time (less than 50ms latency) immersive stereoscopic 3D visuals. Some units were also networked together for a multi-player gaming experience

- **1995:** Virtuality Group Arcade Machines: The Virtuality Group launched a range of arcade games and machines. Players would wear a set of VR goggles and play on gaming machines with real-time (less than 50ms latency) immersive stereoscopic 3D visuals. Some units were also networked together for a multi-player gaming experience

- **2012:** Oculus Rift Kickstarter is launched and backed. Oculus would later be bought by Facebook for $2 billion

- **2014:** Google Cardboard released.

- **2015:** The HTC Vive was unveiled during HTC's Mobile World Congress keynote in March 2015. Development kits were sent out in August and September 2015, and the first Consumer version of the device was released on April 5th, 2016.

- **2016:** Google Daydream was announced.

- **2018:** At the Facebook F8 Developer Conference, Oculus revealed the Half Dome – a headset with a 140-degree field of vision

7.2 How VR works, hardware and software

There are basically 2 types of Virtual Reality technologies:

- Cave Automatic Virtual Environment (CAVE)
- Headset Technologies

CAVE: The Cave Automatic Virtual Environment (CAVE) is a video theater situated within a larger room. The walls of a CAVE can be made up of

- rear-projection screens, or
- flat panel displays

The projection systems are very high-resolution due to the near distance viewing which requires very small pixel sizes to retain the illusion of reality. The user wears 3D glasses inside the CAVE to see 3D graphics generated by the CAVE. People using the CAVE can see objects floating in the air, and can walk around them, getting a proper view of what they would look like in reality. This is made possible by the use of infrared cameras. CAVE user's movements are tracked by the sensors typically attached to the 3D glasses and the video continually adjusts to retain the viewers perspective. Computers control both this aspect of the CAVE and the audio aspect. There are typically multiple speakers placed at multiple angles in the CAVE, providing 3D sound to complement the 3D video.

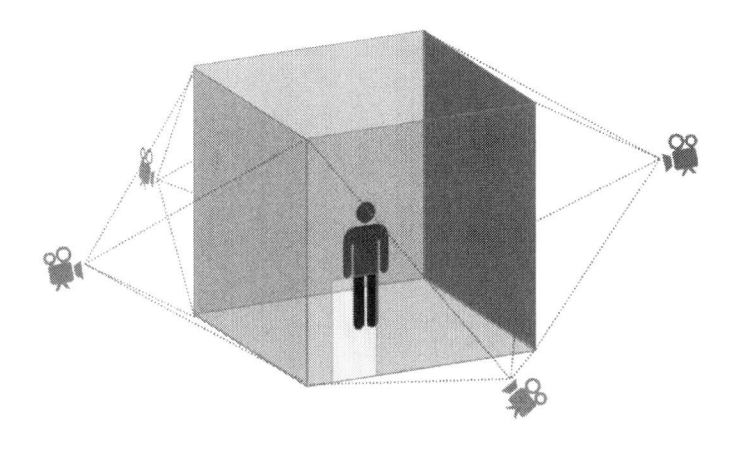

Figure 17: Pictorial representation of CAVE technology[56]

Headset Technologies: Headset Technologies are more familiar to the big public as it provides a cheaper solution to experience VR. Headsets comprise a stereoscopic head-mounted display (providing separate images for each eye), stereo sound, and head motion tracking sensors (which may include gyroscopes, accelerometers, structured light systems, etc.) Base on their tracking method, Headset technologies can be divided in 2 main categories:

- **DoF:** Tracking will track how the headset is rotated, so it will know where we're looking. Most mobile VR platforms use 3DoF tracking. Inertial Measurement Units (IMUs) are

---

[56] https://www.themarketingtechnologist.co/virtual-reality-connecting-unity-to-the-cave/

used to track the rotation. IMUs use a gyroscope, accelerometer and a magnetometer to detect rotations. All modern 3DoF tracking uses an IMU.
- **6 DoF:** It will track rotation PLUS position. It will know where we're looking and where we are in the world. This is how high-end VR systems, like the HTC Vive and Oculus Rift, allow you to move around the room. There are many different ways to accomplish 6DoF tracking. The Oculus Rift uses a large number of LEDs and external cameras that build a model and then it tries to fit a 3D model of the headset with the 2D model it sees of the camera. Then it uses information from an internal IMU to calculate head position. The HTC Vive uses infrared lasers to measure the time it takes to sweep vertically and horizontally across a photo sensor. It uses the data it gets and an internal IMU to determine where your head and hands are located.

Another classification of VR Headset-based technologies is:

- **Mobile VR:** Mobile VR uses IMU tracking, so it only has 3DoF tracking. It can only track your head's rotation – not it's position. It's also "untethered", meaning that there's no wires connecting your headset to a computer. You can use it anywhere. It has less powerful graphics and is powered by a battery.
- **Desktop VR**: Desktop VR uses 6DoF tracking and is typically tethered. It's plugged into a computer and uses the computer to do the graphics work and to get its power. The graphics are generally more impressive. Most

desktop VR headsets also come with hand controllers that allow for more interactivity and a more immersive experience.

A very popular VR set is provided by HTC, the HTC Vive, which are already widely used in big companies for different purposes:

The HTC Vive starter kit, for example, is composed by the following hardware:

1 Headset:

- Screen: Dual AMOLED 3.6'' diagonal
- Field of view: 110 degrees
- Sensors: SteamVR Tracking, G-sensor, gyroscope, proximity

2 Controllers:

- Sensors: SteamVR Tracking
- Input: Multifunction trackpad, Grip buttons, dual-stage trigger, System button, Menu button

2 Base stations

- IR laser grid emission
- 360-degree play area tracking coverage

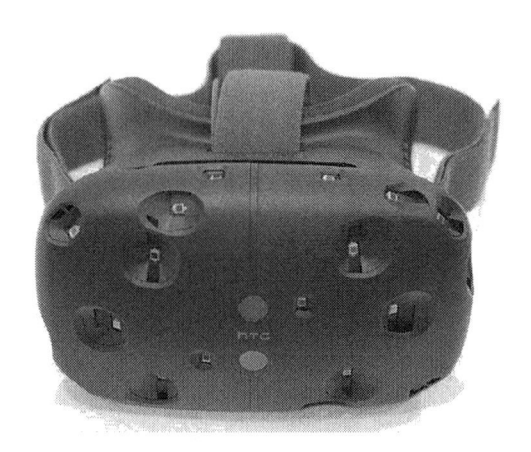

Figure 18: HTC Vive Headset

However, there is another super cheap way to experience VR with mobile VR based technologies. Indeed, you can buy Google Cardboard for about 10 $ on Amazon, for example. Then, what you have to do is to put your smart mobile inside the Cardboard and launch a VR experience. It's plenty of App you can download for free, but also you can watch Youtube videos in VR!

Headset-based VR Development: generally, developing for VR requires writing some code, using an editor, or a combination of both. An editor, or game engine, is a software development framework that makes it easier to develop games. Game engines typically provide 3D rendering, physics, sound, scripting, animation, asset management, and more. This will enable us to develop quickly and learn. Other popular game engines are:

- Unreal Engine
- Cryengine
- Lumberyard

You can also use native development tools like OpenGL and Microsoft DirectX. These options offer more flexibility, but typically have much longer development times and writing more code. WebVR is also an option. However, it's not yet good enough for production apps.

CAVE VS Headset Technologies

In my professional career I had the opportunity to try both solutions. My preferred solution is the Headset Technology for different reasons:

- it is much cheaper compared to a CAVE implementation
- the virtual experience is different: the CAVE provides probably a more realistic experience, while the Headset is like being in a videogame. From my point of view is difficult to say which is better. Personally, I prefer the Headset solution
- Portability. A CAVE is fixed, while the headset is portable

7.3 Main benefits, limitations and applications of VR

Main Benefits

- Risk mitigation assessment in an immersive environment for an experience close to real life.
- Safe environment to experience situations without risks.
- Low cost technology, compared to physical training.
- Gamification helps in the learning process.

Main Limitations

- Gravity can´t be experienced: during a training session, for example, the gravity effect can play a major role (e.g. lifting objects).
- People are not familiar with this technology; therefore, they are reluctant in investing even a minimum budget for VR.

Main Applications

- **Training**: as already mentioned, this is probably the main application for VR. Aerospace companies are already using this solution for MRO training.

- **Factory planning**: a VR simulation provides an engaging and low risk environment to test solutions and scenarios before capital investments.
- **Product Development Assessments**: VR provides a more realistic environment rather than assessing 3D models on a computer.
- **Marketing**: more and more companies are offering VR to advertise their products in trade fairs

Chapter 8: Big Data Analytics

8.1 Brief History 161

8.2 What Big Data are 162

8.3 Types of big data and main sources 163

8.4 Analytics of Big Data 167

8.5 Main Benefits of Big Data Analytics 172

8.6 Big Data Analytics requirements and challenges 174

Chapter Summary

"Information is the fuel of the XXI Century and Data Analytics the combustion engine"

Peter Sondergaard, Former EVP, Research & Advisory at Gartner

In this chapter, we will describe what Big Data is, what the main sources of Big Data are, how to take advantage if it with Big Data Analytics and what the main techniques are. Finally, we will present some key requirements and challenges in exploiting Big Data Analytics properly.

Keywords: Big Data, Big Data Analytics, Data Mining, Machine Learning, Artificial Intelligence

8.1 Brief History

- **2005:** Roger Mougalas, director of market research at O'Reilly Media, coined the term Big Data. In the same year (2005), Yahoo created the now open-source Hadoop with the intention of indexing the entire World Wide Web. Today, Hadoop is used by millions of businesses to go through colossal amounts of data.

- **2009:** In the largest biometric database ever created, the Indian government stored fingerprint and iris scans of all of its citizens.

- **2010:** During a speech at the Techonomy, Eric Schmidt, Executive Chairman of Google from 2001 to 2015, presented that there were 5 exabytes of data stored since the beginning of time up to the year 2003.

- **2016:** 5 exabytes are produced every 2 days.

8.2 What Big Data are

Big Data can be described by the following characteristics:

1. **Volume:** the quantity of generated data. The size of the data determines whether it can be considered big data or not.
2. **Variety:** the type and nature of the data. This helps people who analyze it to effectively use the resulting insight. Big data draws from text, images, audio, video; plus, it completes missing pieces through data fusion.
3. **Velocity:** in this context, the speed at which the data is generated and processed to meet the demands and challenges that lie in the path of growth and development. Big data is often available in real-time. Two kinds of velocity related to Big Data are the frequency of generation and the frequency of handling, recording, and publishing.
4. **Veracity:** it refers to the data quality and the data value. The data quality of captured data can vary greatly, affecting the analysis accuracy.

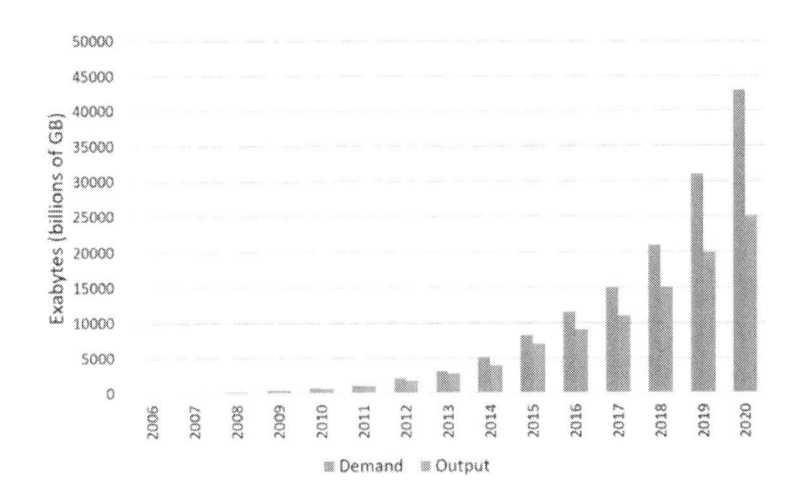

Figure 19: Storage supply and demand from 2006 to 2020[57]

8.3 Types of big data and main sources

Big Data may be classified as either structured or unstructured:

1. **Structured data:** structured data are highly organized and made up mostly of tables with rows and columns that define their meaning. Examples are Excel spreadsheets and relational databases

---

[57] https://www.eetimes.com/author.asp?section_id=36&doc_id=1330462

2. **Unstructured data:** unstructured data is basically everything else

According to a statistic provided by EETimes, the growth of structured versus unstructured data over the past decade shows that unstructured data accounts for more than 90% of all data:

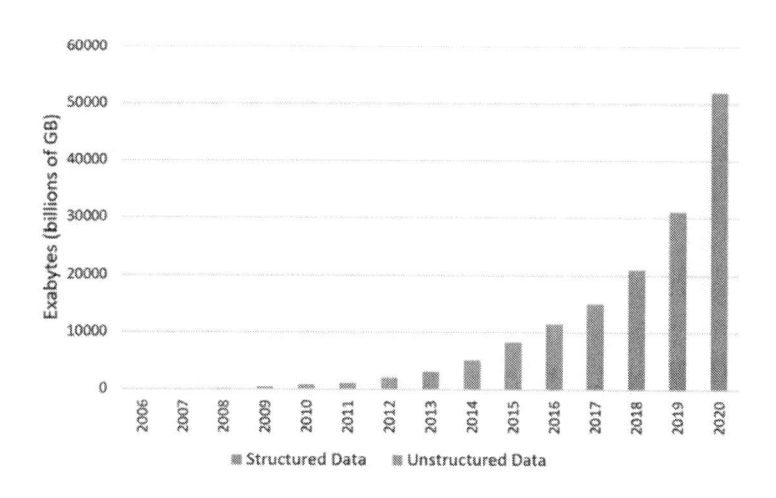

Figure 20: Explosion of digital data from 2006 to 2020[58]

The discrepancy that the observant reader will have noted regarding the value of Exabytes per year in the previous two charts is due to the different sources.

---

[58] https://www.eetimes.com/author.asp?section_id=36&doc_id=1330462

8.3.1 Big Data main source

Big Data comes from:

- **Archives**: scanned documents, medical record, correspondence, forms, insurance etc.
- **Docs**: XLS, PDF, CSV, DOC, HTML, XML email etc.
- **Media**: Images, Video, audio, flash, podcasts, live streams etc.
- **Data Storage**: SQL, NoSQL, Cloud etc.
- **Business App**: Project Management, Productivity, ERP, MES, PLM, etc.
- **Public Web**: Government, traffic, finance, car insurance
- **Social Media**: Twitter, LinkedIn, Facebook, Google+, Instagram etc.
- **Machine Log Data**: event logs, server data, audit logs, mobile location, mobile app etc.
- **Sensor Data**: Medical devices, smart devices, car sensors, road cameras, satellite traffic recording devices, machinery, video games, assembly lines etc.

Focusing purely on the operational industrial context, Big Data comes mainly from:

1. **Cyber-Physical Systems (CPS):** Cyber-Physical Systems have been described in the IoT chapter. CPS are the essence of IoT and IIoT. There are several ways to connect physical assets, for example through RFIDs, or Ethernet,

WLan and so on. Almost all solution implies to exploit digitalization. In this sense, physical systems embed cyber systems, becoming cyber-physical systems (CPS). CPSs transmit a huge amount of data in real-time, such as:
- Logistics & asset tracking data
- Kinematics data from robots and CNC machines
- Temperature control data
- Warehouse management data
- Key Process Variable (KPV) data

2. **Point Cloud Generation Systems:** a point cloud is a set of data points in space generally produced by 3D scanners, which measure a large number of points on the external surfaces of objects around them. Point clouds are used for many purposes, including to create 3D CAD models for manufactured parts, for metrology and quality inspection, and for a multitude of visualization, animation, rendering and mass customization applications. Optical systems are nowadays quite common in industry and their application is fastly growing.

3. **Computer-Aided Engineering (CAE) Systems:** CAE is a category of computer software to aid in engineering analysis tasks. It includes finite element analysis (FEA), computational fluid dynamics (CFD), multibody dynamics (MBD), durability and optimization. CAE areas covered include:

- Stress analysis on components and assemblies using Finite Element Analysis (FEA);
- Thermal and fluid flow analysis Computational fluid dynamics (CFD);
- Multibody dynamics (MBD) and Kinematics;
- Analysis tools for process simulation for operations such as casting, molding, and die press forming.
- Optimization of the product or process.

8.4 Analytics of Big Data

Big Data Analytics can be grouped into 4 main families:

- **Data Science:** data science is an umbrella of several techniques that are used for cleansing, preparation and final analysis of data. It includes data analytics, software engineering, data engineering, machine learning, predictive analytics, business analytics, and more. Unlike data mining and data machine learning, it is responsible for assessing the impact of data in a specific product or organization[59].

[59,58] https://www.datasciencecentral.com/profiles/blogs/difference-of-data-science-machine-learning-and-data-mining

- **Data Analytics:** data analytics implies the use of different technique such as descriptive statistics, data visualization data communication for conclusions. Data analysts must have a basic understanding of statistics, a very good sense of databases, the ability to create new views, and the perception to visualize the data. Data analytics can be referred to as the basic level of data science: a data scientist creates questions while a data analyst finds answers to the existing set of questions[60].

- **Data Mining:** Data mining primary goal is to extract information from various sets of data in an attempt to transform it in proper and understandable structures for eventual use. Data mining can be also seen as a confluence of various other fields like artificial intelligence, pattern recognition, visualization of data, machine learning, statistical studies and so on. While data science focuses on the science of data, data mining is concerned with the process of discovering newer patterns in big data sets. Unlike machine learning, algorithms are only a part of data mining.[61]

So, what is the difference between Data Analytics and Data Mining? Actually, the border is a bit blurry: we can say that Data Analytics has its roots from business analytics or business intelligence models while data

---

[60] https://www.simplilearn.com/data-science-vs-data-analytics-vs-machine-learning-article

mining uses more of scientific and mathematical techniques to come up with patterns and trends, although the goal is basically the same, which is to extract information from Big Data.

In Industry, statistical tools are commonly used to extract data to understand processes and improve them.

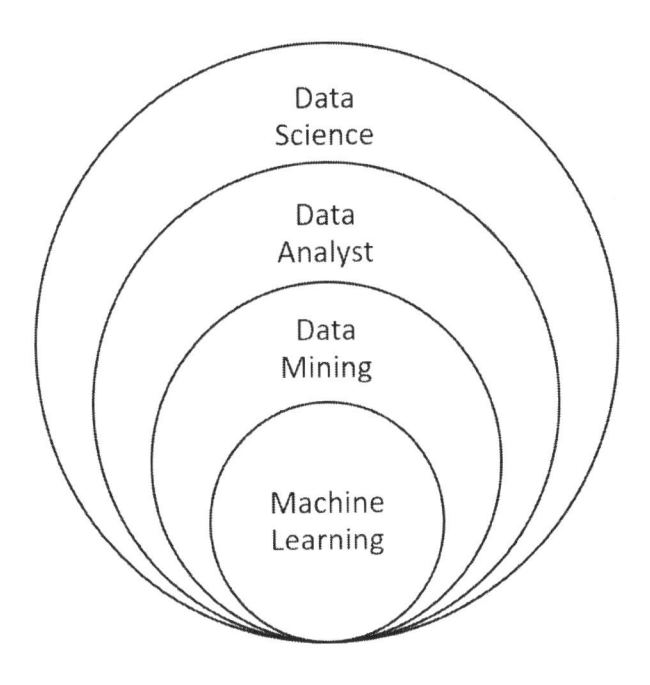

Figure 21: Levels of Data Science

Six Sigma (6σ) is a set of techniques and tools, mainly statistical, for process improvement. It was introduced in 1986 by Bill Smith, an engineer working at Motorola. In 1995 Jack Welch, CEO at General Electric, made it central to his business strategy. In a Six Sigma process, 99.9999998027% (+/- 6 Standard Deviation – Sigma) of parts are statistically expected to be free of defects. Six Sigma strategies seek to improve the quality of the output of a process by minimizing variability in manufacturing and business processes.

- **Machine Learning:** machine learning is kind of artificial intelligence that is responsible for providing computers the ability to learn about newer data sets without being programmed via an explicit source. In machine learning, algorithms are used for gaining knowledge from data sets. Compared to data mining, machine learning mainly focuses on algorithms. When Amazon recommends "You might also like" products, or when Netflix recommends a movie based on past behaviors, machine learning is at work.

Artificial Intelligence (AI) is intelligence demonstrated by machines, in contrast to the natural intelligence displayed by humans and other animals. AI is a branch of computer science that aims to create intelligent machines, and nowadays it has become an essential part of the technology industry. Everyone has certainly experienced AI at least once in his or her life, few examples are:

- **Siri:** Siri is the virtual assistant part of Apple Inc.'s iOS, WatchOS, macOS, HomePod, and tvOS operating systems.

The assistant uses voice queries and a natural-language user interface to answer questions, make recommendations, and perform actions by delegating requests to a set of Internet services.

- **Cortana:** Cortana is a virtual assistant created by Microsoft for Windows 10, Windows 10 Mobile, Windows Phone 8.1. Invoke smart speaker, Microsoft Band, Surface Headphones, Xbox One, iOS, Android, Windows Mixed Reality, and Amazon Alexa. Cortana can set reminders, recognize natural voice without the requirement for keyboard input, and answer questions using information from the Bing search engine.

- **Computer chess:** Computer chess is a game of computer architecture encompassing hardware and software capable of playing chess autonomously without human guidance. Computer chess acts as solo entertainment (allowing players to practice and to better themselves when no sufficiently strong human opponents are available), as aids to chess analysis, for computer chess competitions, and as research to provide insights into human cognition. Current chess engines are able to defeat even the strongest human players under normal conditions. Nevertheless, it is considered unlikely that computers could ever solve chess due to its high level of complexity.

- **Google Translate:** Google Translate uses Google Neural Machine Translation (GNMT), a neural machine translation (NMT) system developed by Google and introduced in November 2016, that uses an artificial neural network to increase fluency and accuracy in Google Translate.

Companies today use machine learning in maintenance and support services. By means of sensors, artificial intelligence helps capture the energy consumption of individual machines, analyze maintenance cycles, and then optimize them in the following stage. Operating data indicates when a part must be replaced or where there is likely to be a defect. As the amount of data increases, the system becomes better at optimizing itself and making more accurate predictions.

8.5 Main Benefits of Big Data Analytics

- **Data-driven decision making:** data mining techniques such as statistics or machine learning can extract useful information from raw data to support the decision-making process. Indeed, data-driven decision making is far more reliable and powerful than just simply opinions.

> *"It is a major mistake to theorize before one has data. One begins to alter the facts to fit them into the theories, instead of theories to fit the facts"*
> Sherlock Holmes

> *"Without Data, you are just another person with an opinion"*
> W. Edwards Deming

- **Understanding and targeting customers:** since marketing is all about reaching the right customers at the right time, Big Data Analytics can be used to predict purchases, analyze customer behaviour. The "you may also like" approach widely use now in almost all e-commerce platform is an example of consumers targeting.
- **Self-optimization:** through machine learning, systems can self-adapt, self-optimize and self-improve to achieve better performances.
- **Security:** cyber-security will have massive benefits in using data analytics techniques. IBM's fraud detection technology helped a large global money-transfer company stop more than $37 million in fraud[62]
- **Smart Factory:** Big Data Analytics is the brain of a Smart Factory: through IoT and CPS, raw data are collected (in the Cloud) and then analyzed through data mining techniques to improve performances.
- **Smart Product Development:** Smart Product Development fosters 4.0 technologies to improve all different stages in the product development process, independently from the method, approach or specific process selected. In the paper "The way from Lean Product Development (LPD) to Smart

---

[62] https://dataflog.com/read/using-big-data-to-improve-law-enforcement/3485

Product Development (SPD)"[63] the authors describe the concept of Lean Product Development as well as new requirements for an intelligent and Smart Product Development through the introduction of modern Industry 4.0 related technologies.

8.6 Big Data Analytics requirements and challenges

- **IT Infrastructure**: a high-performance IT infrastructure must be created. Managing Big Data implies transfer, store, and analyze them.
- **High-speed and reliable Internet connection**: the "always connected" state becomes absolutely a must.
- **Data Storage**: the storage capacity must be adequately provided.
- **Computing Power**: the number of operations per unit of time. Big Data requires by high computing power.
- **Cybersecurity**: this is a recurring topic throughout the entire book. We met cyber-security talking about Internet of Things and Cloud Storage, in which data are collected and then stored to be further analyzed.
- **Skilled data scientist**: first of all, being a data scientist implies having a high-level education (Master or PhD) in

---

[63] Rauch E, Dallasega P, Matt D T, The way from Lean Product Development (LPD) to Smart Product Development (SPD), 26th CIRP Design Conference, Procedia CIRP 50 (2016) 26 – 31

technical fields. The most common fields of study are Mathematics and Statistics (32%), followed by Computer Science (19%) and Engineering (16%). A degree in any of these courses will give you the skills you need to process and analyze big data[64].

Another important aspect is the knowledge of some of the most powerful analytical tools:

- **Python Coding**: is the most common coding language required in data science roles, along with Java, Perl, or C/C++. Python is a great programming language for data scientists. Because of its versatility, you can use Python for almost all the steps involved in data science processes. It can take various formats of data and you can easily import SQL tables into your code. It allows you to create datasets and you can literally find any type of dataset you need on Google.
- **SQL Database Coding**: even though NoSQL and Hadoop have become a large component of data science, it is still expected that a candidate will be able to write and execute complex queries in SQL. SQL (structured query language) is a programming language that can help you to carry out operations like add, delete and extract data from a database. It can also help you to carry out analytical functions and transform database structures.

---

[64] https://www.kdnuggets.com/2018/05/simplilearn-9-must-have-skills-data-scientist.html

- **Apache Spark**: Apache Spark is becoming the most popular big data technology worldwide. Apache Spark is specifically designed for data science to help run its complicated algorithm faster. It helps in disseminating data processing when you are dealing with a big sea of data thereby, saving time. It also helps data scientist to handle complex unstructured data sets. You can use it on one machine or cluster of machines.

Chapter 9: The Cloud

9.1 Brief History 179

9.2 Benefits 180

9.3 Limitations 183

9.4 Service Models 184

9.5 Industrial applications of Cloud Computing 195

Chapter Summary

The Cloud (or Cloud Computing) *"is where software applications, data storage, processing power and even artificial intelligence are accessed over the Internet from any kind of computing device"*. In practical terms, the cloud is made up loads of giant data centres – also known as "server farms" – run by Google, Amazon, Microsoft, IBM, Apple and a host of other traditional and emerging computing giants.

In this chapter, we will describe what the main benefits and limitations of using cloud solutions are and main service models. Finally, industrial applications of cloud computing will be presented.

Keywords: Cloud, Cloud Computing, SaaS, PaaS, IaaS

If you are using popular applications such as Google Docs to create documents, Dropbox to share big files, iCloud to back up your iPhone or Hotmail to check your mailbox, in most cases you are not using a software installed in your PC, but probably a web browser is the only installed software you need. Moreover, data are physically stored in some server somewhere owned by a provider, but it is in most cases irrelevant. This is probably one of the main reasons why cloud computing is so scary and resisted in many corporate data centres. But on the other hand, it is also why cloud computing is so powerful for the vast majority of applications.

9.1 Brief History

- **2006:** Amazon popularized the term "cloud computing" and created subsidiary Amazon Web Services (AWS). AWS is a subsidiary of Amazon that provides on-demand cloud computing platforms to individuals, companies and governments, on a paid subscription basis. The technology allows subscribers to have at their disposal a virtual cluster of computers, available all the time, through the Internet.

- **2008:** Google released Google App Engine (GAE) in beta. GAE is a web framework and cloud computing platform for developing and hosting web applications in Google-managed data centers.

- **2010:** Microsoft released Microsoft Azure, a cloud computing service created by Microsoft for building, testing, deploying, and managing applications and services through a global network of Microsoft-managed data centers.

- **2012:** Oracle announced the Oracle Cloud. This cloud offering is poised to be the first to provide users with access to an integrated set of IT solutions, including the Applications (SaaS), Platform (PaaS), and Infrastructure (IaaS) layers.

- **2013:** Google Compute Engine was released. Google Compute Engine is the Infrastructure as a Service component of Google Cloud Platform which is built on the global infrastructure that runs Google's search engine, Gmail, YouTube and other services. Google Compute Engine enables users to launch virtual machines on demand.

9.2 Benefits

- **Security, Privacy and Reliability:** *"From the perspective of a hacker… it is infinitely easier for me to break through the meagre security on a personal computer than it is for me* *to take on a Google server"*[65]. Security issue may be accounted for contractually. For example, in October 2009 Los Angeles City Council decided to move its 30000 employees to Google's Government Cloud services and a security-breach penalty clause was added to the contract.

- **Device Independent:** data and applications are accessible from any connected computer. If you are working on a project using Google docs, for example, you don't have to worry if the computer on which you are working contains the most recent version of the file. If you lose your laptop or if your hard disk brakes, your work is still in the cloud, and you can continue to work on another device.
- **High collaborative:** co-workers are always sure they are working on the latest version. It doesn't matter if they are all based in different places, different countries or continents, as long as they are connected, they can always collaborate on the same updated file.
- **Task centric:** the cloud is focused around what users want to achieve, rather than any particular software, hardware or network infrastructure.
- **Dynamically scalable:** any user can draw as many or as few computing resources from the cloud as they require at any particular moment.
- **Democratization:** *"Cloud computing can deliver CAE to the masses with minimum investment. Start-ups or small companies can access an incredible deal of computing*

---

[65] Barnatt C, A Brief Guide to Cloud Computing: An essential guide to the next computing revolution. (Brief Histories) Little, Brown Book Group. Kindle Edition, 2010

power to run demanding simulations." –Dominique Lefebvre, head of Product Management at ESI Group

- **Cost savings:** in most cases, cloud solutions are free, nobody is paying or is expecting to pay to open a mail account or to use Google Docs. The Telegraph Media Group, for example, expects to reduce its software costs by 80% over 3 years following its switch from local Microsoft software to Google Apps
- **No fixed costs:** traditionally, computing involves substantial fixed costs, which includes the cost of building, equipping and maintaining data centres, as well as software licenses and customer support. Cloud computing is dynamically scalable and task-centric, and for most users it has no fixed costs. Rather, all costs are on a per-usage or variable basis.
- **Environmentally friendly:** the world's data centres already have about the same carbon footprint as the airline industry. Compared to in-house or desktop computing, cloud computing uses server providers which can run their infrastructure more efficiently. With about half of the energy used by a large data centre going into cooling, putting cloud server farms in very cold countries would be a wise choice, saving money and carbon footprint. In preparation for its anticipated cloud computing "cold rush", Iceland is laying high-capacity, fiber optic cables to connect the country with North America and Europe.

9.3 Limitations

- **Reliable and high-speed internet connection:** all the benefits listed in the previous section have no meaning if an internet connection is not available. Moreover, high-speed connection is in most cases required where power computing is demanding.
- **Regulations:** in some specific situations, regulations may limit the use of Cloud Computing. For instance, Export Control Regulations. Export control regulations are international laws that prohibit the unlicensed export of certain commodities or information for reasons of national security or protections of trade. Export controls usually arise for one or more of the following reasons:
    - The nature of the export has actual or potential military applications or economic protection issues.
    - Government concerns about the destination country, organization, or individual.
    - Government concerns about the declared or suspected end use or the end user of the export. Export Control plays a role as soon as sensitive documentation is exported in another country, including sending email through servers located in different countries.
- **Cybersecurity:** although it is true that the Cloud can be considered a safe environment for most of the application, we can't say the Cloud in 100% safe. There is

still a small probability that a cyberattack will be successful. Therefore, for all these situations where high-confidential information is shared, Cloud can be still risky. In Business, high-confidential information may include Intellectual Property (IP). In this case, a separate storage (such as portable hard disk or pen drive) is still probably the best option.

9.4 Service Models

There are essentially 3 ways in which a business may replace traditional in-house systems with cloud computing (see Figure 22):

- Software (and Storage) as a Service (SaaS)
- Platform as a Service (PaaS)
- Infrastructure as a Service (IaaS)

All involve a cloud vendor supplying servers on which their customers store data and run applications.

When companies choose SaaS, they can only run those applications that their supplier has to offer. If they opt for PaaS, they can create their own applications but only in a way determined by their cloud supplier. And last, when they opt for IaaS, they can run any applications they want on cloud hardware of their own choice.

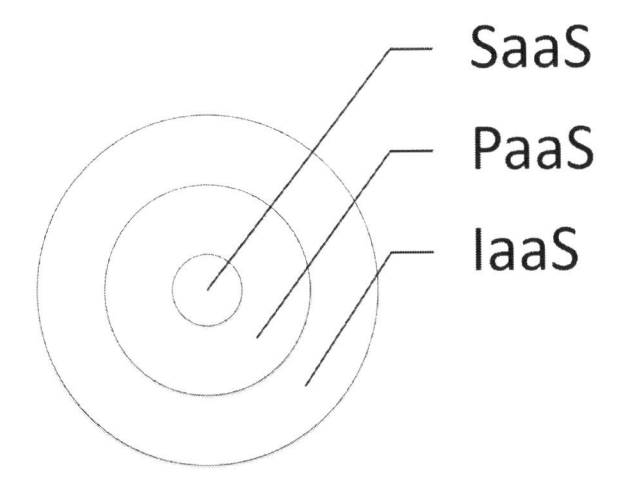

Figure 22: Service models in Cloud Computing

9.4.1 Software as a Service (SaaS)

Software as a Service (SaaS) *"is the technical term for a computer application that is accessed over the Internet instead of being installed on a computer or in a local data centre"*[66]. As already mentioned, one of the main benefits of SaaS applications is to be accessible from any device, including home PC, work PC, netbook, tablet or smartphone.

---

[66] Barnatt C, A Brief Guide to Cloud Computing: An essential guide to the next computing revolution. (Brief Histories) Little, Brown Book Group. Kindle Edition, 2010

Applications include:

- **SaaS E-Mail:** most of you probably now use free on-line e-mail service, such as Gmail, Yahoo! Mail or Windows Live Hotmail. Another option is to install an e-mail application, such as MS Outlook. When people use on-line services, their messages never leave the cloud, and the e-mail software used to write and read the message is also never installed on user's PC.
- **Office SaaS:** almost everyone needs traditional office application such as a word processor or a spreadsheet, which are also available as a cloud-based office package, typically for free. All the following examples are Microsoft Office compatible:

    - **Google Docs**: the suite consists of a word processor, spreadsheet and PowerPoint presentation application, coupled with an online storage service
    - **Google Suite**: it includes Gmail, Google Calendar, Google Video, the Google Sites website and intranet creation tool and loads of storage space
    - **Zoho**: it contains word processing, spreadsheets, presentations, databases, note-taking, wikis, web conferencing, customer relationship management, project management, invoicing, and other applications
    - **Acrobat**: Adobe created its own suite which includes pdf creator, a cloud-based file sharing and storage, a web conferencing tool called ConnectNow, a word

processor (Buzzword), presentations package (Presentations) and a spreadsheet (Tables)
- **SlideRocket**: it is an online presentation package for high-professional presentations and far more sophisticated than any of its SaaS competitors

- **SaaS Desktop:** some companies now deliver cloud-based operating system and a desktop on which run them:
  - **ZeroPC**: it provides a Windows-like desktop loaded with a word processor, spreadsheet, presentations package and other applications, including, for example, a pdf reader, media player and messaging application
  - **EyeOS**: it is an opensource SaaS Desktop
  - **IT Farm**: it provides a paid service where standard Microsoft Office and other Windows Packages are installed on their servers and delivered via a web browser. It is like running a cloud-based copy of Windows

- **SaaS Photo and Video Editing**
  - **Photoshop Express**: it is an on-line version of the Photoshop image editing package. Registration is for free;
  - **Pixlr**: in contract to Photoshop Express, Pixlr looks and behaves like the traditional full version of Photoshop running in a web browser

- **SaaS Business Applications**

Most of the SaaS applications I have listed so far cover almost all needs for home users, but to run a business something different maybe is required:

- **Zoho Creator**: this application has been previously introduced when Office SaaS was described. Zoho has also a business software application called Zoho Creator. It can be thought of as a web-based version of Microsoft Access, but from a certain point of view even more powerful because it offers the ability to create online databases that can be used simultaneously by many company's employees or customers.
- **Salesforce**: Salesforce CRM Sales is a popular sales management application
- **Employease**: it provides human resource information systems that allow companies to run their payroll, benefits administration and other personnel-related IT in the cloud
- **Clarizen**: it describes itself as providing "online work management software for companies". It offers project-management application that can be collaboratively used to manage resources, timesheets, budgets or expenses
- **Netsuite**: it claims to be "the first and only online business application to support an entire company". It offers tools for Customer Relationship Management

(CRM), Enterprise Resource Planning (ERP), e-commerce and website management.
- **WebEx WebOffice**: it is a suite of online collaboration tools. The applications allow people to hold virtual meetings by using phone conferencing, share documents and share desktops

9.4.2 Storage as a Service (SaaS)

SaaS has the same acronym as Software as a Service. It provides the facility to store, share and back up files on the Cloud. Popular services include:

- https://www.box.com
- https://www2.livedrive.com/
- https://www.dropbox.com/
- https://www.icloud.com/
- https://onedrive.live.com
- https://www.google.com/drive/

9.4.3 Platform as a Service (PaaS)

Platform as a Service enables to access online hardware in a software environment in which companies can develop and run their own SaaS applications. PaaS vendors provide everything necessary to create, test and deliver new online applications. Possibilities ranges from the development of new business systems for a particular organization, through the development of online customer interfaces using PaaS tools to help bring new SaaS applications to market. For example, Google offers a PaaS service called App Engine. App Engine allows anybody to write new cloud applications and to deliver them over the web using Google's infrastructure.

One of the major advantages of many PaaS offerings is that new applications do not have to be migrated between systems. It is therefore unlikely that a new application that has been properly tested will not work perfectly the moment it goes live on the web. However, PaaS is not a perfect solution. One of the biggest potential drawbacks of developing new applications using PaaS is vendor lock-in. There are currently a relatively small number of PaaS vendors available, and all of them have their own standards and programming tools. Therefore, users inevitably become reliant on their chosen vendor, making the choice of vendor critical, and is likely to drive most users to the doors of large organizations like Google and Microsoft.

Other PaaS providers are:

- **Force**: this is the PaaS offer from Saleforce.com. It allows anybody to build and run applications on the same infrastructure used for Salesforce's off-the-shelf SaaS applications

- **Microsoft Windows Azure**: Azure is Microsoft's platform for running Windows applications and storing data in the cloud.

Technically speaking, also online website builders fall into the PaaS category:

- Google Sites
- Moonfruit
- Wix
- Webs
- WordPress

9.4.4 Infrastructure as a Service (IaaS)

"IaaS is where a vendor offers computer hardware in the cloud on which their customers can store data and develop and run whatever applications they please. IaaS therefore allows companies to move their existing programs and data into the cloud and to close down their own local servers and data centres"[67]

The fundamental building block of computing infrastructure is the server, which can be defined as a piece of hardware that offers remote processing power and/or storage capacity.

---

[67] Barnatt C, A Brief Guide to Cloud Computing: An essential guide to the next computing revolution. (Brief Histories) Little, Brown Book Group. Kindle Edition, 2010

Servers that can be accessed over the Internet are therefore what IaaS vendors supply to their customers.

Servers are expensive hardware for the following reasons:

- constantly need power supply;
- need great deal of cooling;
- need a secure environment to protect them from fire or other natural disaster;
- must be backed up regularly;
- need 24/7 IT support to ensure they work properly and to effect repairs if necessary.

For these reasons, IaaS is a convenient solution for SME, startups and any business that can't afford a data centre. On the other hand, cloud computing servers must be connected with robust, high-speed connection. Although few years ago servers could be associated with a physically discrete hardware box, today it is not true anymore. Indeed, most servers consists server blades built in racks. A rack is an equipment stand, usually around 50cm wide, on which a number of server computers can be stored. Today the racks in most large data centres contain blade servers. Basically, a blade server is a computer circuit board with a processor, memory and a hard drive or two attached. The benefit of blade servers is that they save a great deal of space and use less energy because each server blade does not need its own, individual power supply. Nowadays modern racks can accommodate up to 128 server blades.

IaaS vendors may rent virtual or real servers, which means that while cloud data centres contain rack upon rack of server blades, these physical servers are subdivided by a software process called "virtualization".

Figure 23: Server Racks[68]

There are currently 4 categories of IaaS services:

- **Private Cloud**: this is potentially the most secure form of IaaS. Physical servers are all located in the same part of a data centre, which means that their cloud hardware is as separated as possible from that of other users

---

[68] https://commons.wikimedia.org/wiki/File:Half_filled_server_racks.jpg

- **Dedicated Hosting**: a customer rent a number of dedicated physical servers within a cloud data centre. Like private cloud, the customer doesn't share their hardware with anybody else, however the customer doesn't have control of the location of its physical server. A benefit of this approach is that it can be dynamically scaled: when the customer needs to increase or decrease the number of servers they are using, they can do that easily even on hourly basis
- **Hybrid hosting**: a customer rents dedicated physical servers, but with virtual servers' instances added into the mix to increase flexibility at minimum cost
- **Cloud Hosting**: a customer can buy as many virtual server instances s required on demand, but there is no control where data are stored and their applications run. They simply share server blades with other customers. Although for some companies this is too risky, cloud hosting is without doubt the most technically and environmentally efficient form of cloud computing. Several companies are now operating in the IaaS marketplace:
    - **Amazon Web Services (AWS)**: Amazon's IaaS is fully virtualized, with the company selling virtual server instances
    - **GoGrid**: it offers cloud hosting, hybrid hosting and dedicated hosting solutions
    - **Rackspace**: it is a well-known provider of traditional hosting services

9.5 Industrial applications of Cloud Computing

In the factory of the future, physical assets like machines, robots, fixture and so on communicate each other and share information at all company levels by means of the cloud. We can imagine a virtual invisible cloud full of data to be shared and analyzed through AI to improve flexibility, quality, efficiency and effectiveness of the production system. Following, some examples of industrial applications are be presented:

- **Work instructions:** manual operations are typically supported by work instructions. "Paperless" supports are becoming more popular for several reasons:
    - paper can be lost, while digital are always stored safely
    - digital work instructions are always up to date
    - they are environmentally friendly, as the use of paper is eliminated
    - videos, links and data input can be used
    - they can be automatically translated in different languages

    Moreover, the use of work instructions in the Cloud adds even more benefits:

- they can be shared throughout different plants, located in different locations
  - the revision alignment is guaranteed

- **Digital platforms:** in December 2016, in the Business section of The Economist the article "Siemens and General Electric gear up for the internet of things" was published. The article deals with two the two similar approaches that these two big companies are using to face up to the Digital Transformation. The answers are called Predix for GE and Mindsphere for Siemens: they are open cloud platform or "IoT operating system" for applications in the context of the Internet of Things. Operational data are stored and made accessible through digital applications to allow industrial customers to make decisions based on valuable factual information. As cloud-based PaaS (platform as a service), they collect and analyze all kinds of sensor data in real time. This information can be used to optimize products, production assets and manufacturing processes along the entire value chain.

- **Virtual teams:** virtual teams are made by people located in different buildings, cities, countries or continents. They may be part of the same organization or they may come from different companies. Virtual teams communicate through digital technologies, using the cloud.

Chapter 10: Simulation

10.1 Introduction 199
10.2 Discrete Event Simulation 200
10.3 Process Simulation 207

Chapter Summary

Simulation tools are fundamental in engineering to predict the behaviour of new products, therefore reducing the associated risks before entering into service. However, if simulation is widely used in Design Departments, however we can't say the same in Manufacturing. In this chapter we will introduce some of the most important simulation tools that are now available to implement new facilities or to optimize existing production lines. In this sense, Discrete Event Simulation is a fundamental tool.

Keywords: Simulation, Discrete Event Simulation, Process Simulation

10.1 Introduction

"Physical testing costs at least five to six times the cost of product development resources on vehicle projects. The only way to meaningfully reduce the cost of physical testing is with simulation."

Dominic Gallello, president of MSC Software.

"The digital manufacturing building is based on simulation processes for testing new ideas and options before actual implementation of these ideas. With simulation models, we can explicitly visualize how an existing operation might perform under varied inputs and how a new or proposed operation might behave under same or different inputs, analyze the material flow and optimize plant lay-out. Today simulation can be used for decision support with supply chain management, workflow and throughput analysis, facility layout design, resource usage and allocation, resource management and process change"[69]

Simulations tools have been traditionally used in the engineering world since decades. Some examples are:

- CAD models, which are normally used as digital mock up to simulate geometries and encumbrances

---

[69] Kokareva V.V. et al, Production Processes Management by Simulation in Tecnomatix Plant Simulation, Applied Mechanics and Materials Vol 756 (2015) pp 604-609

- CAM systems, which are used to simulate machining processes, typically the tooling path
- Multiphysics simulations, which are usually numerical implemented with discretization methods such Finite Element Method, Finite Difference Method, and Finite Volume Method. Many software packages mainly rely on the finite element method or similar commonplace numerical methods for simulating coupled physics: thermal stress, electro- and acoustic- magneto mechanical interaction

10.2 Discrete Event Simulation

A Discrete-Event Simulation (DES) models the operation of a system as a discrete sequence of events in time. Each event occurs at a particular instant in time and marks a change of state in the system. Between consecutive events, no change in the system is assumed to occur; thus, the simulation can directly jump in time from one event to the next. DES is a popular decision support tool, often used to enhance understanding of interactions within the simulated system, and identifying system issues (e.g. bottlenecks and long lead times) and solutions. A DES study starts with the building of a virtual model of a physical system, current or future, and then simulating and analyzing the results of the virtual model to gain insights into the physical system. DES is commonly used for the simulation of dynamic systems (e.g. manufacturing and supply chains).

A Discrete Event Simulation is an effective approach for a confident decision making based on data and experiments. Simulation is able to answer critical questions to different levels:

- **Plant designer**: how to satisfy the expected performance of the system for the client?
- **Plant manager**: how to adapt the production system to new products & improve it?
- **Production manager**: how to optimize the production plan? Impacts of the changes in the line?

A DES can also provide important support in different phases in manufacturing. In Table 7 you can see what type of support a DES can provide during the design phase, reconfiguration phase and production planning phase.

	Design	**Reconfiguration**	**Production Planning**
Main aspects	Capacity Capex Flexibility Utilization	Reconfig. Costs Utilization Reconfig. Time	Operational Costs Inventory Deadlines Reliability
Simulation Model	High Fidelity Analysis Uncertainty Different designs	Existing conditions Systems evolutions Different designs	Production Status Customer orders Shopfloor conditions

Table 7: How DES can support different phases in manufacturing

In the design phase, some of the main aspects to take under considerations are the production capacity, the capital expenditure (capex), the flexibility that a production system should guarantee and utilization of machines and workers. In this phase, a DES is able to provide high fidelity analysis of different designs, substantially reducing the associated uncertainty.

The reconfiguration phase occurs when changes must be introduced in our production system, due to the introduction of new products or to an increase in capacity or to optimize the system. In this phase, DES is an important tool to model existing conditions and evolutions, as well as to explore different options.

In the production planning phase, a DES is able to calculate with extreme accuracy operational costs, verify if deadlines can be met, therefore verify how reliable the production system is to fulfill customer expectations.

In Figure 24: Block scheme of a Discrete Event Simulation process steps a methodology to conduct a DES study is proposed. These 14 stages provide the foundation to construct an informative and validated DES model, while ensuring the model meets the customer needs.

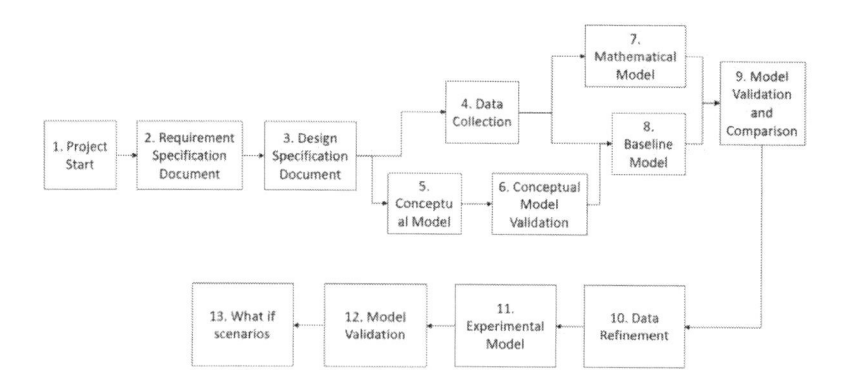

Figure 24: Block scheme of a Discrete Event Simulation process steps

A short description of each stage is provided below:

1. Project start: initial meetings to discuss requirements and scope of study and gain understanding of current process

2. Requirement specification document: capturing exhaustive and prerequisite details to understand and verify project requirements

3. Design specification document: specifying the logic and behaviour of simulation model and verifying the customer

4. Data collection: collecting of what data is available, both numerical and behavioral, which is needed for construction of the model

5. Conceptual model: defining of process flow diagram which shows how the model will be structured and how it will behave

6. Conceptual model validation: validating the conceptual model with the customer to ensure that all the data and processes are captured before model development can start

7. Mathematical model: creating of a mathematical model based on the collected data. This includes outputs such as expected processing times and number of reworks and is used as an internal validation tool for the DES model, checking model results against expectations from the raw data

8. Baseline model creation: creating of a baseline DES model to reflect the current state of the facility

9. Model validation / Test plan: validating and verifying the model using the mathematical model and with input from the customer

10. Data refinement: updating the data and behavior in the model according to new data or time and motion studies that have been performed

11. Experimental model: using the updated data, and customer feedback to update the DES model into a form suitable to explore scenarios;

12. Model validation: validating experimental DES model with the customer. Completion of this stage implies that the model is frozen, and no data will change;

13. "What-if" scenarios: using the experimental DES model to produce results for scenarios of interest that have been agreed upon by the customer

According to Kokareva et al.[70], main benefits for the production planner include:

- enhance productivity of existing production facilities by as much as 20%
- reduce investment in planning new production facilities as much as 30%
- cut inventory and throughput time by as much as 40%
- optimize system dimensions, including buffer sizes
- reduce investment risks through early proof of concept
- maximize use of manufacturing resources
- improve line design and schedule

Different tools are available on the market, but the most popular are:

- Tecnomatix Plant Simulation by Siemens
- Witness by Lanner
- DELMIA by Dassault Systeme
- Simul8 by Simul8 Corporation
- Flexsim by FlexSim Software Products, Inc

---

[70] Kokareva V.V. et al, Production Processes Management by Simulation in Tecnomatix Plant Simulation, Applied Mechanics and Materials Vol 756 (2015) pp 604-609

10.3 Process Simulation

In addition to Discrete Event Simulations, the market offers several tools to simulate in very detail each step of a process. At the beginning of this chapter, we have already mentioned some common tools used in manufacturing like CAM simulations or Multiphysics simulations.

Another type of simulation which is also recommended to analyze the overall process is the Process Simulation. One of the most common digital tools in this sense is called Process Simulate by Siemens Process Simulate is a digital manufacturing solution for manufacturing process verification in a 3D environment. Main features include:

- Static and dynamic collision detection
- Sequencing of operations
- Assembly and robotic path planning
- Line and workstations design
- Human tasks simulation, like reach envelopes, vision window, postures, ergonomics analysis
- Robot-related simulation, like reach test, process simulation, programming, logic editing and validation
- Virtual commissioning

Main benefits of Process Simulation are:

- Reduce cost of change with early detection and communication of product design issues

- Reduce number of physical prototypes with upfront virtual validation
- Optimize cycle times through simulation
- Ensure ergonomically safe processes
- Reduce cost by re-using standard tools and facilities
- Minimize production risk by simulating several manufacturing scenarios
- Early validation of the mechanical and electrical integrated production processes (PLC and robotics)
- Increase process quality by emulating realistic processes throughout the process lifecycle

Chapter 11: Horizontal & Vertical IT Systems Integration

11.1 Introduction 211
11.2 Horizontal IT Systems Integration 214
11.3 Vertical IT Systems Integration................................ 217
11.4 Inter-Organizational IT Systems Integration............. 218

Chapter Summary

With Industry 4.0, companies, departments and functions will become much more cohesive, as cross-company, universal data-integration networks evolve and enable truly automated value chains. In this chapter, a short glimpse on IT systems and benefits on their integration within the company and the supply chain will be provided.

Keywords: IT systems integration, horizontal integration, vertical integration, inter-organizational integration

11.1 Introduction

Organizations have traditionally been structured around business functions, supported by individual IT systems, using most of the time different applications and technologies, such as programming languages or protocols.

However, today's trends are changing: competitive businesses need high level of integration among all divisions. Therefore, IT support must not be restricted to a single business function, but cut across many different functional areas. These trends require for the integration of current functionality-oriented systems, and this integration needs to be delivered within short time[71]. In the factory of the future, networking and interconnectivity are key components, therefore intra-organizational and inter-organizational cooperation and communication will increase significantly. Workers will collaborate and communicate without borders by using smart devices which connect them in real-time to their co-workers and workplace tools as needed.

Figure 25 shows the 3 main levels of an organization:

- Shopfloor it is the lowest level. Operations, Supply Chain, Quality, Design Manufacturing Engineering are typically involved

---

[71] Gehrke L. et al, A Discussion of Qualifications and Skills in the Factory of the Future: A German and American Perspective, VDI and ASME, April 2015

- Organization and planning are the intermediate level where organizational activities at all functional levels are performed
- "Standards" is the highest level, where company standards are defined and strategic decisions are taken

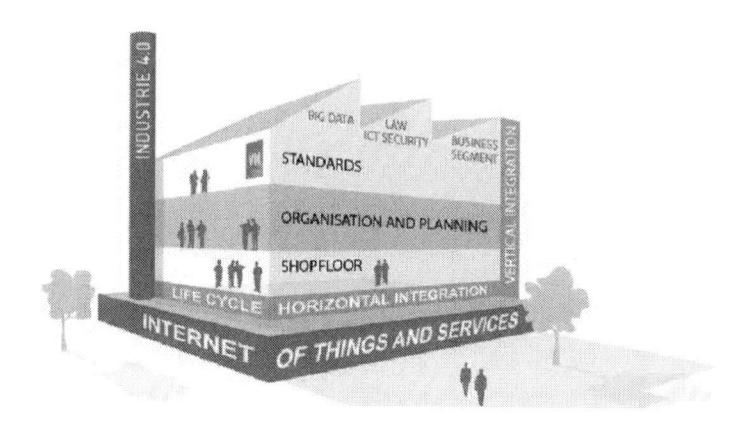

Figure 25: Vertical and Horizontal integration under Industry 4.0[72]

The product portfolio of an organization IT department is becoming wider and wider:

- HR typically uses dedicated applications to manage employees payslips, career path and similar activities

---

[72] Gehrke L. et al, A Discussion of Qualifications and Skills in the Factory of the Future: A German and American Perspective, VDI and ASME, April 2015

- Design Engineering uses CAD, Simulation and PLM software to design and manage products
- Manufacturing Engineering uses similar software, including CAM to program NC machines and MES to interface with Operations
- Quality Engineering uses PLM and dedicated software to manage Quality documentation
- Operations uses MES systems to manage everyday activities and ERP to plan workloads
- Supply Chain uses applications to manage material and keep relationships with suppliers
- Customer Support has specific applications to manage relationship with customers
- Program Management and Planning use specific software and applications, usually ERP and PLM are shared with other divisions

These are only some examples of applications required by different departments in a mid-large organization. Some software solutions already integrate different functionalities: for example, ERP systems embed functionalities of MES and PLM systems and vice versa.

A high level of integration and data-exchange imply several benefits:

- data becomes easily available at different organization levels
- better data driven decision making
- less management costs

- less time spent in retrieving and collecting data
- less complexity in managing interconnectivity between different systems
- higher efficiency

11.2 Horizontal IT Systems Integration

Horizontal System Integration implies the integration of IT systems at the same organization's level. According to Wangler and Paheerathan *"a typical example of horizontal integration is Supply Chain Management, in which an organization tries to optimize the complete set of activities of order entry, purchasing, production, shipment etc to minimize lead time and costs for production and at the same time maximize value for the customer"*.[73]

Another concrete example is the production environment. Operations is the core of manufacturing companies selling products:

- in modern organizations, concurrent design and manufacturing activities are required to make better, faster and cheaper products. CAD and PLM (Product

---

[73] Wangler B., Paheerathan S J, Horizontal and vertical integration of organizational IT systems, Information Systems Engineering, The Pennsylvania State University, 2000

Lifecycle Management) software are typically involved in this process
- once the product has been designed, it is necessary the design and implement the proper method of manufacturing and assembly. CAD, CAM, PLM and MES software are commonly used, as well as ERP to other dedicated tools to plan and buy materials and contact suppliers to perform purchase orders. In parallel, a Quality Plan must be deployed
- Parts are then produced following the manufacturing and assembly routes released by MES tools.

A Product Lifecycle Management system (PLM) is a business computing solution that aims to manage the entire life cycle of the product on a single computing platform: from the time it is created and designed, through the prototype phase, first pre-series, manufacturing and maintenance-after-sales service. A PLM system coordinates how people create and use product information in their daily processes.

A Manufacturing Execution System (MES) is a software tool that functions as an extension of the ERP system, but oriented to the planning and execution of production. In this way, while the ERP system determines what has to be manufactured, the MES system provides the necessary functions for the management of key areas in a plant, such as people, materials, processes, quality, traceability and maintenance.

An Enterprise Resource Planning (ERP) is the integrated management of core business processes, often in real-time and mediated by software and technology. ERP provides an integrated and continuously updated view of core business processes using common databases maintained by a database management system. ERP systems track business resources—cash, raw materials, production capacity—and the status of business commitments: orders, purchase orders, and payroll. The applications that make up the system share data across various departments (manufacturing, purchasing, sales, accounting, etc.) that provide the data. ERP facilitates information flow between all business functions and manages connections to outside stakeholders.

It is evident that the integration of aforementioned tools may simplify otherwise complex activities and make the data and information flow smoother. Some organizations think that expensive ERP like PeopleSoft, SAP, Baan, etc. may support better the inter-process chain integration, but this is actually not true for 2 main reasons:

- there is no ERP solution that will provide all the functionality an organization requires
- there is always a tendency to maximize the return of past investments on information systems

11.3 Vertical IT Systems Integration

Vertical System Integration means the integration of IT systems to support the information flow through all administrative levels of an organization. An example is the data flow required for production: *"frequently different operating systems and networking technologies are used. These systems need to be fed with control data stemming from higher level planning and scheduling systems while the lower level applications need to collect data and pass them upwards"*.[74]

Operations has the primary role to produce the amount of parts (throughput) required by the organization with assets and instructions provided by Manufacturing Engineering Department. The final outcome can be:

- keep asset portfolio and the number of workers (considering specific skills as well) as-is
- improve capabilities by investing money in R&D and new machines
- improve capacity by purchasing new state of the art machines

---

[74] Wangler B., Paheerathan S J, Horizontal and vertical integration of organizational IT systems, Information Systems Engineering, The Pennsylvania State University, 2000

This type of analysis is normally performed at the intermediate level, while decisions are taken at the top level. Therefore, it is evident how important is to guarantee the proper data flow in both directions (top-down and bottom-up). Typical tools used to manage data flow throughout all different organization's levels are ERPs, MESs and PLMs.

11.4 Inter-Organizational IT Systems Integration

Enterprises need to exchange information in order to collaborate and negotiate. For example, an organization needs to contact suppliers to provide the required assets (e.g. tools, fixtures, machines and so on) against a purchase order from a customer. *"Supply chain logistics and fulfillment companies integrating with their customers' fulfillment and shipping systems, or financial services firms integrating with retailers of financial products are just few more examples of this multi-enterprise integration".*[75]

Since different companies use different tools, systems and platforms, the key issue in inter-organizational integration is to get the data of one application of an organization matching

---

[75] Wangler B., Paheerathan S J, Horizontal and vertical integration of organizational IT systems, Information Systems Engineering, The Pennsylvania State University, 2000

with another application of another organization. There are 2 main ways to achieve this purpose:

- use the same tool or platform. Some examples are:
    - in the supply chain is the use of Electronic Kanban Systems
    - use file/data sharing platforms

- use same data standards and protocols:
    - use same CAD formats
    - use same data protocols. For example, in the gear industry, Gear Data Exchange (GDE) is becoming a sensitive topic

Chapter 12: Cyber-security

12.1 Brief History 221

12.2 Top 5 most notorious cyber-attacks 222

12.3 Basic concepts 225

12.4 Defense methods 229

Chapter Summary

"If you are not concerned about cybersecurity, you don't know enough about it."[76]

Cyber-crime is now the fastest-growing industry on the planet, with estimated revenues of $445 billion in 2016, according the World Economic Forum.

In this chapter, we will present some notorious cyber-attacks in history and we will introduce you to basic principles of cybersecurity. In the last section, we will provide you some practical defense methods against cyber-attacks.

Keywords: cyber-security, cyber-attacks, malwares

[76,69] Meeuwisse R, "Cybersecurity for Beginners", Cyber Simplicity Ltd; 2nd edition (March 14, 2017)

12.1 Brief History

- **1983:** Cyber-security begins together with Internet: as soon as PC started to be connected each other, hacking was possible. However, at the dawn on internet connection, the speed was much slower than it is today and it costed a fortune. Moreover, the probability to be infected by viruses was fairly small, and the maximum consequence was just to re-install files. The key factor that gave rise to cybersecurity threats was that Internet connection speeds became faster, cheaper and more widely adopted. This change, together with faster computer processing speeds and better web application programming, gradually made it easier, more effective and cheaper to provide mainstream services through the Internet, rather than using traditional offline routes.

- **2005:** Until this date, the IT hardware and software were controlled by the company IT department and technologies operated almost exclusively within the internal company network. Then, the Cloud arrived: indeed, in chapter 9 we learnt that Amazon launched its Cloud service (AWS) in 2006. Apple with their iPhone and App Store contributed with the change in thinking. It was clear for companies that, applying a similar philosophy, they would have more choices, greater flexibility and lower costs. This change in scenarios drastically changed the role of IT technologists: they will focus more on cybersecurity to guarantee safety and reliability of IT tools, reducing vulnerability that might be leveraged (vulnerability is "a weakness that could be compromised and result in damage or harm").

12.2 Top 5 most notorious cyber-attacks

- **WannaCry**: the WannaCry attack put ransomware, and computer malware in general, on everyone's map, even those who don't know a byte from a bite. The four-day WannaCry epidemic knocked out more than 200,000 computers in 150 countries. This included critical infrastructure. In some hospitals, WannaCry encrypted all devices, including medical equipment, and some factories were forced to stop production.
- **NotPetya / ExPetr:** the worm moved around the Web, irreversibly encrypting everything in its path. Although it was smaller in terms of total number of infected machines, the NotPetya epidemic targeted mainly businesses, partly because one of the initial propagation vectors was through the financial software MeDoc. The damage from the NotPetya cyberattack is **estimated at $10 billion**, whereas WannaCry, according to various estimates, lies in the $4–$8 billion range.

- **Stuxnet:** nothing could match Stuxnet for complexity or cunning — the worm was able to spread imperceptibly through USB flash drives, penetrating even computers that were not connected to the Internet or a local network. The worm manifested itself only on computers operated by Siemens programmable controllers and software. On landing on such a machine, it reprogrammed these controllers. Then, by setting the rotational speed of the uranium-enrichment centrifuges too high, it physically destroyed them.

- **DarkHotel:** on connecting to a hotel network, they were prompted to install a seemingly legitimate update for a popular piece of software, and immediately their devices were infected with the DarkHotel spyware, which the attackers specifically introduced into the network a few days before their arrival and removed a few days after. The stealthy spyware allowed the cybercriminals to conduct targeted phishing attacks.

- **Mirai**: devices whose security had never been considered and for which no antiviruses existed suddenly began to be infected on a massive scale. These devices then tracked down others of the same kind, and promptly passed on the contagion. This zombie armada, built on a piece of malware romantically named Mirai (translated from Japanese as "future"), grew and grew, all the while waiting for instructions. Then one day — October 21, 2016 — the owners of this giant botnet decided to test its capabilities by causing its millions of digital video recorders, routers, IP cameras, and other "smart" equipment

In 2014, Ofcom[77] reported that average UK adult spent more time per day using digital devices (8h and 41 min) than sleeping (8h and 21 min). The main reason is that smart devices make people more powerful: nowadays it is almost impossible to get lost by using google maps, it is simple to check and book restaurants nearby, check and make transactions on bank account, find information easily googling everything and so on. Now a personal question: are you aware of the type and amount of information that your web accounts save? I recently discover it by myself setting my Google account and I was astonished. So, if you are curious, please have a look. The question is: are these technologies 100% secure?

---

[77] https://www.ofcom.org.uk/__data/assets/pdf_file/0031/19498/2014_uk_cmr.pdf

12.3 Basic concepts

In his book "Cybersecurity for Beginners" [78], Meeuwisse describes the steps to build an effective cybersecurity system:

- **Identify your valuable asset:** to apply the proper level of security, it is necessary to understand that the value of different types of information determines how much protection it requires. Classifying our information lets us know what to defend, but we still need to understand where to defend it. The cyber defense points are the digital locations where we could add cybersecurity controls. Typically, 6 layers of digital defense points are identified:
  - **Data**: any digital information
  - **Devices**: computers, smartphones, tablets, USB drives are just some examples
  - **Applications**: any programs/software installed in a device
  - **Systems**: group of applications that work together to serve a more complex purpose
  - **Networks**: a group of devices that are connected together physically (by wires) or virtually (using applications)
  - **Other communication channels:** CD-ROM drives, USB ports, wi-fi, Bluetooth etc.

---

[78] Meeuwisse R, "Cybersecurity for Beginners", Cyber Simplicity Ltd; 2nd edition (March 14, 2017)

- **Protect with appropriate security**: 4 major categories of security controls can be identified. The following list ranks them form the safer to the less effective:
    - **Physical**: put information to restricted equipment, physically separated. Examples are digital memory card, a USB drive and so on
    - **Technical**: the use of a digital method to command how something can or cannot be used. Removing the ability to cut or paste information on a smartphone is an example of a technical control that can be used to minimize security risks
    - **Procedural**: instructions during a sequence of required steps to limit how something is or is not permitted to be used. An example is to require a minimum of 2 authorized people to approve any access
    - **Legal**: the use of legislation to help promote and invest in positive security methods and also to deter, punish and correct infringements.

- **Detect, respond, recover:** it implies the detection of any compromised account or device, quarantine the problem and identify countermeasures and recover by replace, restore or fix compromised assets. There are 3 main control modes to protect a digital device:
    - **Preventive controls**: it protects the device before an event happens

- **Detective controls**: it monitors and alerts me if something happens
- **Corrective controls**: it rectifies any gaps after the problem has been identified

12.3.1 Human factors

"People are regarded as the weakest link in cybersecurity"[79]

The most significant human factors are:

- **Inadequate cybersecurity knowledge**: cybersecurity is not a static discipline and an ongoing and substantial personal investment is required to stay up to date
- **Poor capture and communication of risks**: people tend to notice but not to report risks (culture and relationship issues)
- **Under-investment in security training**: it results in a low level of awareness and management
- **Using trust instead of procedures**
- **Absence of a single point of accountability**, the principle that all critical assets, processes and actions must have clear ownership and traceability to a single person

---

[79] Meeuwisse R, "Cybersecurity for Beginners", Cyber Simplicity Ltd; 2nd edition (March 14, 2017)

- **Social Engineering** is the art of manipulating people through personal interaction to gain unauthorized access to something

12.3.2 Threats

What are main threats and how they can attack us? In the cyber-security context, main threats are malwares and they can enter in our systems through the attack surface. The attack surface is the sum of the different points where an unauthorized user ("attacker") can try to enter data into or extract data from an environment. The six layers of digital defense points are the attack surface.

Malwares: a malware is a malicious software, such as a virus, which is specially designed to disrupt or damage a computer system. A virus is a form of malware that spreads by infecting to other files and usually seeks opportunities to continue that pattern. Malwares are typically used to:

- infect, which means to create damage or disruption
- steal information
- take instruction from the attacker
- steal confidential information
- steal money from a bank account
- block the user's access until a ransom is paid (ransomware)

12.3.3 Types of malwares

- Phishing is using an electronic communication (e.g. email) that pretends to come from a legitimate source, in an attempt to get sensitive information (e.g. a password or a credit card number) from the recipient or to install a malware on the recipient's device
- Spear phishing is a more evolute form of phishing. It describes the use of an electronic communication that targets a particular person or group of people and pretends to come from a legitimate source
- Polymorphic malwares are malicious software that can change its attributes to help avoid detection by anti-malware

12.4 Defense methods[80]

12.4.1 Basic

- **Install an effective anti-malware:** a computer program designed to look for specific files and behaviors that indicate the presence or the attempted installation of malicious software

---

[80] Meeuwisse R, "Cybersecurity for Beginners", Cyber Simplicity Ltd; 2nd edition (March 14, 2017)

- **Install a Firewall**: hardware or software used to monitor and protect inbound and outbound data by applying a set of rules (the firewall policy)
- **User Access Control**: rules and techniques used to manage and restrict entry to or exit from a physical, virtual or digital area through the use of permissions
- **Data retention and destruction**: a non-technical strategy which means to destroy data following certain criteria. An easy example of this principle is email: after a certain period of time, emails will be deleted
- **Password Management**
    1. **Use strong passwords**: according to security experts, using a chain of 4 or 5 random words in lower case letters is thousands of times more difficult to crack than a password with 8 characters that contains combinations of numbers, special characters and upper- and lower-case letters. This because password-cracking software are educated about human password patterns: password guessing software can start by expecting that the first character is a capital letter and the last character is most likely to be a special character or set of numbers,
    2. **Change Passwords regularly**
    3. **Access to every single online service with a different username and password**. Indeed, almost every service requires its own username and password, and instead of using different usernames and passwords, many people follow the unsafe practice of re-using the same ones. This means that instead of cracking

passwords, criminals can process long lists of historic usernames and passwords into automated software that can check if they work in thousands of different online services.
- **Create high-security zones**: create high-security zones that add substantially more protection to the most sensitive data. Sometimes closed system are used (not connected with a public network)
- **Implement segmentation**: to reduce security risk, a method is to subdivide the attack surface using network segmentation, which means splitting a collection of devices and applications that connect, carry or safeguard data into smaller sections. This allows for more discrete management of each section, allowing greater security to be applied in sections with the highest value, and also permitting smaller sections to be impacted in the event of a malware infection or other disruptive event
- **Timely patch management**: A controlled process used to deploy critical, interim updates to software on digital devices
- **Regular backup**: Regular back-up is a key process that can allow computer systems to be restored in the event of a successful attack.
- **Establish a Computer User Policy**: And educate users to a good security practice

12.4.2 Advanced

- **Multi-factor authentication:** this means using more than one form of proof to confirm the identity of a person or device attempting to request access (fingerprint, face recognition)
- **Encryption/Cryptography**: the art of encoding messages so that they cannot be read by anybody who intercepts them
- **Proxy servers**: programs used to provide intermediate services between a requested transaction and its destination. Proxy servers enhance security by hiding exact information about locations and users in a particular network. Attackers frequently use proxy servers for the same goal
- **Penetration testing**: it checks and scans on any application, system or website to identify any potential security gap (vulnerabilities) that could be exploited. The process can involve hackers that a company pays to manually try to identify security weaknesses. There are also automated tools that can perform similar assessments
- **Vulnerability assessment**: the identification of security gaps in a computer, software application, network or other section of a digital landscape
- **Create Honeypots**: they are electronic devices or collection of data that are designed to trap would-be attackers by detecting, deflecting or otherwise counteracting their efforts. The honeypot will contain

nothing of real value to the attacker, but will contain tools to identify, isolate and trace any intrusion

Chapter 13: Other Technologies

13.1 Smart Human Machine Interface............................235

13.2 The Digital Twin...240

13.3 Blockchain...245

Chapter Summary

In the previous chapters, we have provided a full description of the key 4.0 technologies identified by the Boston Consulting Group. However, other smart technologies are available on the market and some of them are becoming more and more popular in different industrial sectors.

In this chapter, we will describe 3 additional technologies or trends that are worth mentioning ad describing more accurately: Smart Human Machine Interface, Digital Twin and Blockchain.

Keywords: Human Machine Interface, Wearables, Digital Twin, Blockchain

13.1 Smart Human Machine Interface

A Human Machine Interface (HMI) is basically a device which interfaces the machine and the operator. The main 4 functions are:

- allow the machine/system to display its status to the operator
- allow the machine/system to display instructions to the operator
- allow the machine/system to display outcomes
- allow the operator to input actions to the machine/system

Although touch screens are widely used especially in machining industry, several different devices can be now used as well. Most of them are part of the "Wearables" category. Typical wearables are glasses, watches/smartphone and gloves.

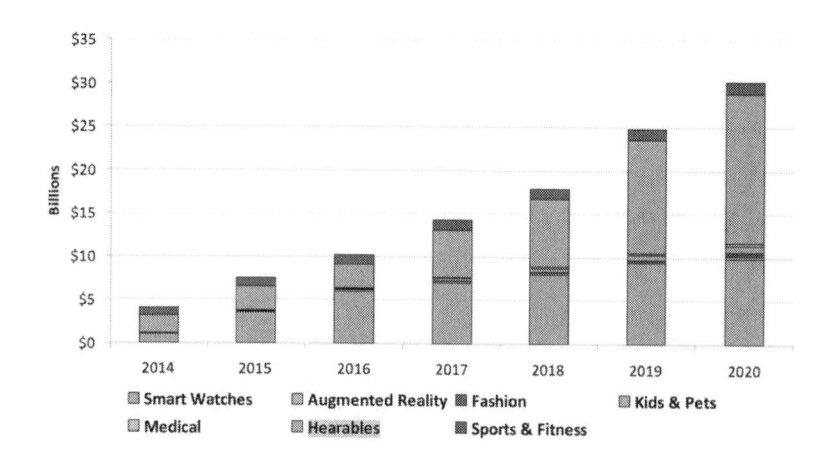

Figure 26: Global Revenue from Smart Wearables and Hearables[81]

Main benefits of wearables are:

- **Hands-free:** workers don't need special devices to handle, for example a scanner gun to scan barcodes, or a monitor to check work instructions or input data. This will increase productivity
- **Safety:** safety information can be displayed or in general communicated to the operator in real time in case of fire or similar events
- **Confirmation technology:** selection of work step confirmation technologies that you need

---

[81] https://commons.wikimedia.org/wiki/File:Global_Revenue_from_Smart_Wearables_and_hearables.png

- **Image recognition:** identification of objects just by the power of sensors
- **Localization and navigation:** navigation and positioning for your frontline worker to stay on track. This might be a problem and it is recommended to agree the utilization of this options with the employer and unions
- **Remote assistance:** a camera embedded on smart glasses allows technicians to provide instructions remotely
- **Live video call:** communication between workers and technical assistance whenever needed
- **Documentation:** transformation of work activities into instant documentation with zero touch
- **Ergonomics:** exoskeletons may reduce significantly health problems due to ergonomic issues
- **Reporting & Analytics:** monitoring of all work being executed by your frontline workers with simple tools

Tablets: Tablets are widely used by people in their everyday life. They combine features of a laptop and portability. Nowadays 2-in-1 laptop may provide basically the same benefits. Tablets can be used by quality supervisors to daily monitor the WIP status, document non conformances, and to connect to machines to monitor their "health". Emails can be immediately sent in case of issues. Special tablets are available for industrial utilization: these tablets are built to survive to specific environment or products (e.g. corrosion protection oil, lubricant, coolant etc.)

Smart Glasses: smart glasses are wearable computer glasses that add information alongside or to what the wearer sees. Like other computers, smart glasses may collect information from internal or external sensors. It may control or retrieve data from other instruments or computers. It may support wireless technologies like Bluetooth, Wi-Fi, and GPS. A smaller number of models runs a mobile operating system and function as portable media players to send audio and video files to the user via a Bluetooth or Wi-Fi headset. Some smart glasses models, also feature full lifelogging and activity tracker capability. Some applications re:

- smart glasses can be used to identify the asset position and scan barcode/ QR code in a warehouse
- more complex solutions can be adopted to display work instructions and guide the operator
- complex smart glasses solutions may provide support for training and designing exploiting a high level of augmented reality

Smartphones and smartwatches: smartphones and smartwatches are small and powerful computers. Attached to an arm or a wrist, are often used by runners to track performances and listen to the music. However, they can be used in a shopfloor environment for all different purposes listed above. Moreover, special apps can be used for additional activities, possibilities are limitless.

Wristbands: Amazon has patented designs for a wristband that can precisely track where warehouse employees are placing their hands and use vibrations to nudge them in a different direction. When someone orders a product from Amazon, the details are transmitted to the handheld computers that all warehouse staff carry. Upon receiving the order details, the worker must rush to retrieve the product from one of many inventory bins on shelves, pack it into a delivery box and move on to the next assignment[82]. Similar solutions are used by the German company Sarissa that developed a Local Positioning System (LPS) which combines advanced ultrasound technology, easy-to-use software and a powerful, open interface architecture. It can be used as a mistake proofing solution to track, for example, if the worker is picking up the right components from a kitting rack.

Exoskeletons: we mention exoskeleton here although it would be more correct to locate them in the Human – Machine – Collaboration category. Anyway, exoskeletons are armor that serve to help operators to maintain prolonged postures and support weight in a more ergonomic way. Some exoskeletons available on the market are:

- **SuitX**, a spinoff of the University of California, develops the so-called modular exoskeleton MAX, consisting of three parts for areas of common injuries in the workplace:

---

[82] https://www.theguardian.com/technology/2018/jan/31/amazon-warehouse-wristband-tracking

Shoulders, Lumbar and Knee. The launch cost is around $3000, varying depending on the units purchased

- **LegX**, a structure that goes from the hip to the feet with regulation of the degree of inclination and that allows the operator, with semi-flexed legs, to reduce the effort to stay standing (the sensation is similar to sitting on a chair) lower back
- **BackX** reduces the weight of the objects that are lifted from the ground by 13 kg
- **ShoulderX** allows you to reduce the effort when supporting weights on the head
- **ExoArm**, developed by two young Slovenian engineers, is an open-source arm at a cost of only 100 €. It has an Arduino heart, and they're trying to program everything with an easy code to understand and modify. They have a first functional prototype capable of lifting weights of 10 kilograms, and the next step will be to improve the design to finally launch it on the market

13.2 The Digital Twin

Digital Twin refers to a digital replica of physical assets, processes, systems and devices. It integrates artificial intelligence, machine learning and software analytics with spatial network graphs to create living digital simulation models that update and change as their physical counterparts' change. A digital twin continuously learns and updates itself from multiple sources to represent its near real-time status, working condition or position. This learning system, learns from itself, using sensor data that conveys various aspects of its operating condition.

13.2.1 Brief History

- **1970**: many authors reported that the concept of a digital twin was first applied during the Apollo 13 program, where engineers on the ground needed to be able to rapidly account for changes to their vehicle while exposed to the extreme conditions in space

- **2003:** the concept of a virtual, digital equivalent to a physical product or the Digital Twin was introduced in 2003 at the University of Michigan Executive Course on Product Lifecycle Management (PLM)[83].

- **2011**: NASA and the US Air Force published two papers on digital twins. They discussed the concept of a digital twin on a structural level to help predict fleet maintenance. These papers are two of the most highly cited documents on the topic, and are recognized as being the first time the phrase was taken seriously by both industry and academia. Subsequently the use of the term declined

---

[83] Grieves M, Digital Twin: Manufacturing Excellence through Virtual Factory Replication, March 2015

- **2016**: the term started spread among the Industry community. More recently, the term has seen a marked increase in search activity, most likely due to the general adoption of the term by industry and marketing teams

13.2.2 Components of a Digital Twin

According to a report by the High Value Manufacturing Catapult Visualisation and VR Forum[84], we can identify the following components of a Digital Twin:

Required:

- **A Model:** a model of the physical object or system, which provides context. The provision of a 3D model is not a requirement for the creation of a digital twin. In some cases, it can add some value, but this value is derived from the capability to derive a greater understanding of the contextualisation of the data presented. However, this is not always the case, and in some cases, a 3D model will be excessive to requirements.
- **Connectivity:** connectivity between digital and physical assets, which transmits data in at least one direction
- **Real-time:** connectivity between digital and physical assets, which transmits data in at least one direction

Optional:

- **Analytics:** the optional logic for a digital twin may (and often will) include rule engines or complex-event processing that are applied to incoming IoT data. These logic elements may generate alerts or triggers that orchestrate workflows and various forms of descriptive analytics to identify when thresholds are exceeded; they can also drive predictive analytics that provide inputs to enterprise stakeholders. A model of the physical object or system, which provides context. The provision of a 3D model is not a requirement for the creation of a digital twin. In some cases, it can add some value, but this value is derived from the capability to derive a greater understanding of the contextualisation of the data presented. However, this is not always the case, and in some cases, a 3D model will be excessive to requirements
- **Control:** not all digital twins will have the ability to control an object but, when they do, they will connect via the object's specific control system. On-board actuators, electronic switches and other digital-to-analog physical devices make up the control systems
- **Simulation:** a sufficiently detailed digital twin may be used by an enterprise to model the current and future behaviour of an object in a variety of conditions and configurations, anticipate failure and optimal operation modes, or identify optimum schedules for operation, refueling or maintenance.

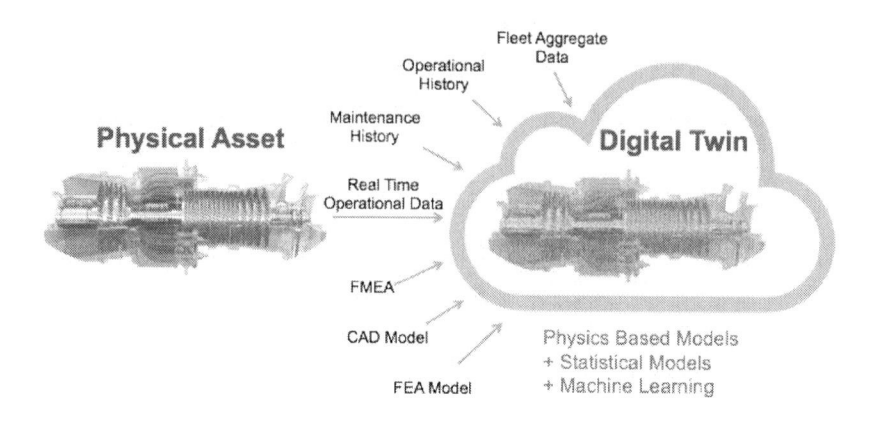

Figure 27: concept representation of a Digital Twin[85]

13.2.3 Some Applications

- **Remote process monitoring**: through the development of digital twin systems, processes can be monitored remotely
- **Remote process controls**: the enablement of control capability from within the digital twin system for remote viewers
- **Predictive analysis**: through the aggregation of historical data, combined with the real time data feed, it is possible

---

[85] https://www.bangkokbankinnohub.com/digitaltwin/

to simulate the future states of production systems, including the development of predictive maintenance models. This enables a great productivity saving through the ability to respond to demand signals rather than either
- **Rapid New Product Development**: through increased customer intimacy greater insight into product or process performance can be developed. This can then be used to influence the next generation developments in physical products or processes.

13.3 Blockchain

A blockchain is a decentralized database; however, this simple definition would leave many people thinking "So what? All that hype for a new type of database?"

Blockchain is not an easy concept to explain, and this is out of scope of this book to enter into too many technical details. In the first chapter of his book "Blockchain: Ultimate guide to understanding blockchain, bitcoin, cryptocurrencies, smart contracts and the future of money ", Mark Gates tries to explain the reason why blockchain is not just a database:

"The common theme from everyday transactions is that we trust the institutions and the centralized databases they maintain to accurately keep a record of our lives. [...] What alternative did people have other than deposit money in what they believed were trustworthy banks and companies? [...] A

decentralized database built on the blockchain removes the need for centralized institutions and databases. Everyone on the blockchain can view and validate transactions creating transparency and trust. Trust lays at the core of the blockchain; it provides a system of trust between people without the need for an intermediary involved in the transactions. The blockchain allows people to transact between each other with anything of value"[86]

13.3.1 Brief History

- **1984**: David Chaum introdeuces the "blind Signature" to guarantee the full privacy of its users. A blind signature is a form of digital signature in which the content of a message is disguised (blinded) before it is signed

- **1990**: David founded DigiCash to create a digital currency

- **1997**: Adam Back proposed Hashcash, is a proof-of-work system used to limit email spam and denial-of-service attacks

---

[86] Gates, Mark. Blockchain: Ultimate guide to understanding blockchain, bitcoin, cryptocurrencies, smart contracts and the future of money. Kindle Edition.

- **1998**: Wei Dai published another paper titled "B-Money, An Anonymous, Distributed Electronic Cash System." The paper outlined the foundations for cryptocurrencies

- **2005**: Nick Szabo proposed Bit Gold, and the idea of Smart Contracts

- **2009**: Bitcoin became more than just an idea in an academic paper when Satoshi Nakamoto created the Bitcoin network along with the first blockchain

13.3.2 How blockchain works

In simple words, in a blockchain-based system, transactions between individuals are associated with a crypted code. In order for a transaction to happen, this code must be decrypted by the miners, who are people in the network who decrypt these codes. The first miner who decrypt the code receives a reward for his effort / work in the form of cryptocurrency (e.g. Bitcoin). This mechanism is called "proof-of-work". The decrypted transaction is then sent to the entire blockchain network to validate the solution and to be recorded in every personal public ledger. When other transactions are decrypted, they are "added" on top of the previous ones, therefore creating a sort of chain (here why the name blockchain). If someone wanted to change an old transaction (block), he should ask to at least 51% of the network to change not only the transaction, but also all following transactions, as they are all linked together. It is evident how difficult this is to make it happen, especially when the network is made of thousands or millions of users. However, this is still considered a risk.

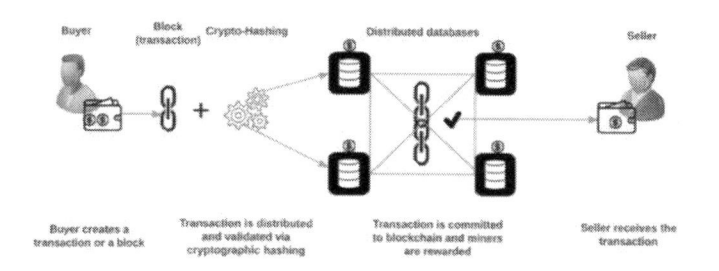

Figure 28: How blockchain works[87]

To summarize the process of how a blockchain-based system works (Figure 28):

- A buyer creates a transaction or a block
- To each transaction (or block), a crypto-hashing is associated
- Transaction is distributed
- Transaction is decrypted by miners
- Miners are rewarded
- The decrypted transaction is recorded into public ledgers

---

[87] https://commons.wikimedia.org/wiki/File:Blockchain-Process.png

- Seller receives the transaction

13.3.3 Smart Contracts[88]

Smart contracts are contracts that are written in computer code and operate on a blockchain or distributed ledger. Smart contracts can be used to exchange anything of value, as mentioned in the chapter about potential uses of the blockchain, many of the industries utilizing blockchain technology will be using smart contracts. When a smart contract is run on the blockchain, it operates automatically. If the conditions of a contract are met, payments or value are exchanged based on the terms of the contract. Likewise, if conditions in the contract are not met, payments may be withheld if written into the smart contract. Smart Contracts are considered to be the most powerful application of blockchain-based systems for both financial and non-financial applications.

---

[88] Gates, Mark. Blockchain: Ultimate guide to understanding blockchain, bitcoin, cryptocurrencies, smart contracts and the future of money. Kindle Edition.

13.3.4 IOTA[89]

IOTA is a cryptocurrency specifically designed for the Internet of things (IoT). Unlike the most popular tokens which are based on proper blockchain architectures, IOTA is based on Tangle: as well as the classic blockchain, Tangle is a distributed network, meaning there is no central instance controlling the currency. Transactions need to create a consensus in order to be validated. In the blockchain one block following the other in a specific order. Tangle, on the other hand, is entirely different. In the blockchain technology there are different possibilities of mining new blocks in order to create a consensus. On the other hand, if someone wants to make a transaction within the Tangle network, this is not necessary. To be able to submit a transaction, you need to approve two other transactions which need to be validated. Some blocks may be confirmed more than one time, as it is based on a random selection. This means that we do not have the distinction between a node, full node and miner. Every node becomes a miner if he wants to make a transaction. Based on this, it allows the user to make 0-transaction-fee transactions. Another benefit is in contrast to the classic blockchain algorithm is that the more people are using a Cryptocurrency like IOTA (Tangle based), the faster the transaction will be transmitted.

---

[89] Kacperczyk, Marcin; Neuefeind, Marvin. Cryptocurrency - A Trader's Handbook: A Complete Guide on How to Trade Bitcoin and Altcoins. Kindle Edition.

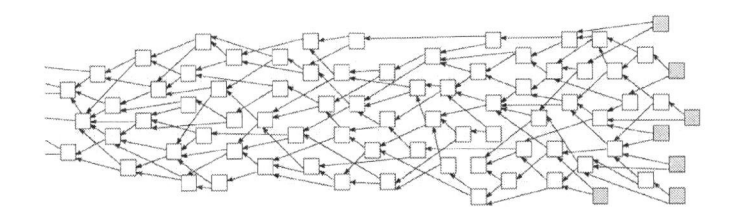

Figure 29: Organization of Tangle blocks[90]

13.3.5 Benefits and challenges

Said that, we can identify some benefits in this process:

- **No intermediaries** (e.g. banks) are required: allowing transactions to occur directly between people instead of involving a third party
- **Transparency**: blockchain provides transparency to all people on the network, with transactions visible to all connected computers
- **Security**: data entered onto a blockchain is immutable, meaning it can't be altered or changed, unless a 51% attack is successful
- **Reduced costs**: blockchain could significantly reduce costs in many industries by removing intermediaries

---

[90] https://commons.wikimedia.org/wiki/File:Tangleimage.jpg

- **Increased transaction speed**: for the same reason, transactions are faster

However, there are also some disadvantages:

- **Energy consumptions**: Professor John Quiggin from the University of Queensland has calculated that every half an hour the Bitcoin network uses the same amount of electricity as the average US household does in an entire year[91]
- **Lack of privacy**: not only is the information not private, but it is also readily accessible at any given moment to anyone using the system
- **Security concerns**: more security can sometimes result in a system being less secure. There are countless examples with cryptocurrencies where someone has forgotten their private key and can't access their money
- **Risk of 51% attack**: if someone were able to control over 50% of the computers on a blockchain network, they would control the transactions on the blockchain
- **Lack of scalability**: at the current rate of energy consumption, the electricity costs of running a blockchain make it unfeasible to handle the number of transactions by credit card companies

---

[91,89] Gates, Mark. Blockchain: Ultimate guide to understanding blockchain, bitcoin, cryptocurrencies, smart contracts and the future of money. Kindle Edition.

13.3.6 Applications

The most common application of blockchain is the creation of cryptocurrencies and financial transactions. However, the development of the so-called Smart Contracts is opening a wide range of opportunities for non-financial applications as well. Some examples are[92]:

- **Identity management and digital identities**: blockchain-based identification systems provide digital signatures using cryptography
- **Healthcare and Medical Records**: storing medical records on a shared database would mean that doctors, hospitals, surgeons, nurses, and health professionals would have access to shared data about a patient at any time, saving time and assisting them to make more comprehensive decisions when treating a patient
- **Academic Certificates:** the blockchain would create transparency around students' academic records and qualifications
- **Cloud Storage**: cloud storage currently requires a lot of trust in third-party companies. Centralized cloud storage systems are vulnerable to attack and passwords can easily be obtained through basic hacking or scamming methods
- **Property & Rental records**: blockchain-based property & rental records and transactions could dramatically

increase the speed and transparency of property transactions while reducing the cost of transactions
- **Logistics and Supply Chain Management**[93]: blockchain enables supply chain to detect counterfeit components, locate the spare parts requiring Maintenance, Repair, and Operations (MRO), and establish the provenance of each part. This is particularly beneficial in industries where transparency and traceability become critical, such as aerospace, military and food industry
- **Enable IoT solutions:** in IoT networks, the exchange of information is critical. Cyber-physical-systems must be able to exchange Information quickly and safely. IOTA has been specifically designed for this purpose.

---

[93] Raja Wasim Ahmada et al, Blockchain for Aerospace and Defense: Opportunities and Open Research Challenges, Computers & Industrial Engineering Journal, November 2020

QUIZ PART 2

1) What are the 2 categories of robot that have been described?

1. Automated Guided Vehicles and Collaborative Robots
2. Collaborative Robots and Autonomous Robots
3. Self-guided robots and Automated Guided Vehicles

2) Describe the Material Extrusion process:

1. The build process starts when a layer of powder is laid on a build platform. A multi-nozzle inkjet print head then travels across the powder bed, selectively jetting a binder solution onto it in the shape of the first object layer. The powder bed is then lowered, another layer of powder is laid down, another layer of binder is jetted onto it, and so on.
2. In Material Extrusion, objects are built up layer-by-layers by putting a semi-liquid material from a computer-controlled nozzle. The most widely extruded materials are thermoplastics that can be temporarily melted for output through a nozzle.
3. In Material Extrusion, a metal powder is directed into a high-power laser beam for deposition as a molten build material

3) What are the 3 ways of working of AR?

1. Artificial Intelligence Based
2. Simultaneous localization and mapping (SLAM)
3. Recognition Based
4. Location based

4) What are the 2 types of VR?

1. Headset technologies and smartphones
2. CAVE based and smartphones
3. CAVE based and Headset technologies

5) What is the Internet of Things?

1. It is a special internet standard to provide a technological platform that enables the development and use of sensors and actuators that can produce and consume enriched sets of data that in turn can be used for economically optimizing industrial automated processes and operations
2. It is the network of devices that contain electronics, software, actuators, and connectivity which allows these things to interact and exchange data
3. It is an internet platform used to support communication among different devices that contain electronics, software, actuators and connectivity

6) Put the 4 layers of Big Data Analytics in the right order, starting from the external layer

1. Data Science
2. Machine Learning
3. Data Analyst
4. Data Mining

7) What are the 4 service models of Cloud Computing?

1. Software as a Service, Platform as a Service, Infrastructure as a Service, Hardware as a Service
2. Storage as a Service, Productivity as a Service, Hardware as a Service, Platform as a Service
3. Software as a Service, Storage as a Service, Infrastructure as a Service, Platform as a Service

8) What are main benefits of a high level of integration and data-exchange?

1. Every Department can have access to other Departments' information without asking for a special authorization
2. Better data-driven decision making
3. Less complexity in managing interconnectivity between different systems

9) Select benefits of Discrete Event Simulation:

1. To identify bottlenecks in advance
2. To reduce process development costs
3. To reduce investment risks
4. To maximize resources

10) What is a Digital Twin?

1. Digital Twin refers to a backup copy of digital models of physical assets of a real Factory
2. Digital Twin refers to a digital mockup of physical assets of a real Factory
3. Digital Twin refers to a digital replica of physical assets, processes, systems and devices

Correct answers:

1) 1 **2)** 2 **3)** 2, 3, 4 **4)** 3 **5)** 2 **6)** 1, 3, 2, 4 **7)** 3 **8)** 2, 3 **9)** 1, 3, 4 **10)** 3

PART 3: THE SMART FACTORY

In Part 2, the 9 key technologies have been described with greater details. We discovered that most of these technologies are not new, but some of them are already quite old, considering the fast pace of technology development we are assisting in these years.

However, a collection of smart solutions is not enough to design and develop a Smart Factory

In Part 3, we will find and answer to the following questions:

1. **What is a Smart Factory?** In chapter 14 a definition and a full description of a Smart Factory will be provided
2. **How to implement a Smart Factory?** First of all, it is important to follow a well-defined and structured methodology. In this sense, chapter 15 will recommend a step-by-step approach.

List of chapters of Part 3

Chapter 14: The Smart Factory 264

Chapter 15: Smart Factory implementation 282

Chapter 14: The Smart Factory

14.1 What is a Smart Factory? 265

14.2 Key word: flexibility 267

14.3 Prerequisites for a Reconfigurable Manufacturing System 269

14.4 Lean Manufacturing 273

14.5 Lean 4.0 274

14.6 Smart Factory and Lights-out manufacturing 279

Chapter Summary

In this chapter, we will describe more in detail what a Smart Factory is. Moreover, we will focus on the key word flexibility: in fact, enabling a reconfigurable manufacturing system is probably the first main requirement in the implementation of a Smart Facility. In this sense, Lean Manufacturing will help to reduce waste and therefore to develop a lean production system. We will describe how Lean will benefit massively from the introduction of 4.0 technologies. Finally, the lights-out manufacturing concept will be introduced.

Keywords: Smart Factory, Reconfigurable Manufacturing Systems, Lean Manufacturing, Lights-out manufacturing

14.1 What is a Smart Factory?

According to Padhi[94], a Smart Factory is

"an optimized manufacturing facility which can

- *facilitate launching new products depending on market dynamics,*
- *is scalable enough to meet demand variation for existing products,*
- *is able to produce Finished Goods at least cost,*
- *has smart machines, sensors and robots which are seamlessly integrated with information system architecture to enable high level of automation in transaction processing and has real time analytics that helps in minimizing downtime and improving efficiency.*

A Smart factory creates an eco-system where there is a strong collaboration between all the key players, e.g. Suppliers, Operations Team, IT Team, Planning Team, Sales & Marketing team and Customers.

It creates a single platform where multiple business functions such as Procurement, Planning, Manufacturing, Sales & Distribution & Finance & Accounting teams work together to meet overall corporate objectives."

---

[94] Padhi N, Setting up a Smart Factory (Industry 4.0)-A Practical Approach, Nov, 2018

Technical basis is Cyber-Physical Systems (CPS), which communicate with each other with the help of the Internet of things (IoT). Part of this future scenario continues to be the communication between the product (e.g. workpiece) and the production plant: the product itself brings its manufacturing information in machine-readable form.

These data are used to control the path of the product through the manufacturing facility and the individual manufacturing steps.

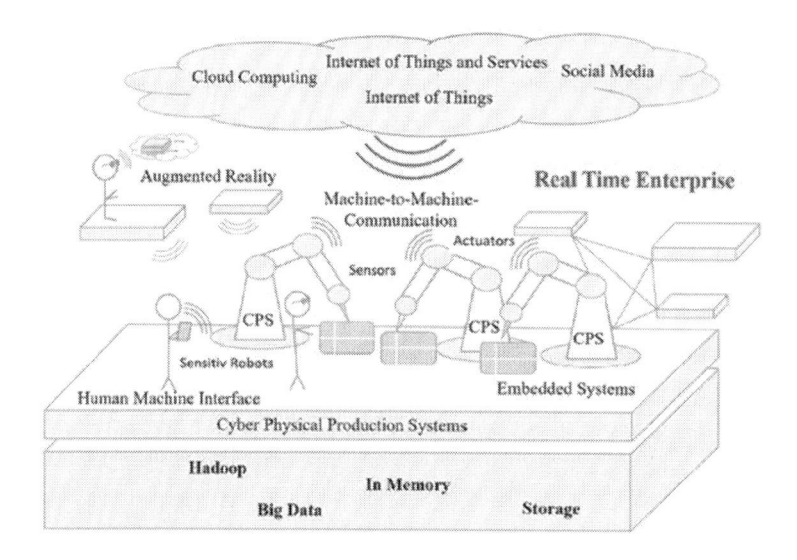

Figure 30: Pictorial representation of a Smart Factory and its technologies[95]

---

[95] Herrmann F, The Smart Factory and its risks, Systems 2018, 6, 38; doi:10.3390/systems6040038

14.2 Key word: flexibility

What's wrong with the production systems of the third industrial revolution? In fact, looking at the productivity of the most industrialized countries in the last decades, this has been increasing progressively. This was possible thanks to new technologies that have allowed ever increasing levels of automation and flexibility.

However, this flexibility does not seem to be enough: to obtain a competitive advantage at a global level, companies must follow the so-called "customer's voice", which requires an ever-greater level of personalization of their products. Just as an example, at the time of writing this book, the BMW plant in Munich (described in more detail in Chapter 7), is producing approximately 1000 cars per day, with such a high level of customization that statistically only 2 cars per month are identical. It is no coincidence that this plant has won several awards for adopting Lean methodologies. How far we are from the black Ford T!

It is easy to understand that, in order to remain competitive, BMW and the other car manufacturers will have to keep up (if not increase) their already high productivity level, and at the same time increase the customization of their models, without increasing the delivery times and associated costs. Furthermore, if the industrialized countries with high labor costs want to rival countries such as China, India or Mexico, just to mention the most important ones, they will have to make sure to eliminate this competitive disadvantage. But how can we obtain a highly efficient system and at the same time guarantee a high level of flexibility, even 1 to 1?

Reconfigurable Manufacturing Systems, or simply RMS, are potentially the answer to managing mass customization, since they can be reconfigured continuously based on market dynamics. RMS make extensive use of digital technologies that guarantee developers low entry barriers. Furthermore, digital technologies have the exact characteristic that modern production systems need: flexibility. A 3D model, for example, can easily be modified, a simulation can be relaunched in a few seconds, a 3D printed component can be modified and reprinted without having to modify the equipment or tools traditionally necessary for its realization.

These technologies will be introduced briefly in the next chapter. However, before going into these issues, it is necessary to present some prerequisites for a reconfigurable production system.

14.3 Prerequisites for a Reconfigurable Manufacturing System

An approach to developing this system is described by Andersen[96], who lists a number of prerequisites:

1. Have a perspective on the life cycle of production systems. In this sense, 3 main challenges are identified:

    - reuse of production equipment: reusing production equipment for new product generations is more complicated than building a new and improved version of the system
    - division of responsibilities between development and production teams: greater integration between these two teams is needed
    - definition of the production system life cycle requirements: predicting potential changes for a period of more than a few years is extremely difficult. This requires management's commitment and involvement as a primary figure to evaluate changing dependent factors strategically

---

[96] Andersen et al, Prerequisites and Barriers for the Development of Reconfigurable Manufacturing Systems for High Speed Ramp-up, 3rd International Conference on Ramp-up Management (ICRM), Procedia CIRP 51 (2016) 7 – 12

2. Correlate the design of the production system with the development of the product portfolio: as in the previous point, this is an extremely complicated task, with elements and situations that simply cannot be foreseen. For this reason, the recommended approach is to plan for everything to be as changeable as possible

3. Have a long-term vision of investments: this is necessary in order to progressively reduce production capacity and to be able to reconfigure the production system

4. Structure your design processes: since designing an RMS involves greater complexity than traditional production systems, it is mandatory to have a structured design process

5. Have a holistic approach: this means including all the functions involved in the production system, including labor, logistics, infrastructure and maintenance, in the process design phase

6. Develop knowledge and skills related to reconfigurability: although it is a fundamental first step for the correct implementation of RMSs, a lack of understanding of what reconfigurability really means is not uncommon

To the points indicated by Andersen, I personally find it useful to add the following:

7. Design of 0 set-up time: it is important to emphasize that the equipment mentioned in point 1 must be designed in such a way as to be reconfigured and reused without interruption, in the most automated way possible.

In the field of mechanical machining, the need for greater flexibility is testified, for example, by the growing market of multi-tasking machine tools. In short, multi-tasking machines combine the characteristics of different machines in a single platform, basically an all-in-one solution. The main advantages are easily listed:

- single set up
- lower footprint
- standard equipment and tools

However:

- higher initial investment is required
- generally, they involve a longer cycle time

Due to the increasing precision that these machines are reaching, multi-tasking machines will become increasingly popular.

Having established what a reconfigurable production system is, we can say that it is a necessary but not sufficient condition for the implementation of a Smart Factory. In this case, the missing element is the concept of autonomy: in general, RMS are not necessarily autonomous. This can be done by implementing Cyber-Physical Systems capable of exchanging information between them through a central system that processes it in real time, thus updating the production system accordingly.

Taking the example of the human body, autonomy, made possible by the development of artificial intelligence and the systems connected to it, represents the brain of the factory, which is able to connect to the nervous system through the use of precise cyber-physical systems and the Internet of Things.

We have arrived at the end of this chapter. We have seen how, in order to remain competitive in the global market, it is necessary to satisfy customer needs by customizing products more while improving quality and reducing costs and delivery at the same time. Reconfigurable Manufacturing Systems promise to be the answer to these needs thanks to the use of new technologies. However, the implementation of these systems requires a series of prerequisites that have been listed by Andersen, to which the need to have extremely short and automated set-up times must be added.

14.4 Lean Manufacturing

We have introduced the term "Lean" as referring to the production system developed by the Toyota Motor Corporation after World War II. Briefly, Lean is a production philosophy that aims to maximize product value by minimizing waste. Some commonly mentioned goals are:

- Improving quality: to remain competitive in the global market, a company must understand the needs of its customers better than its competitors and implement adequate design processes to meet these expectations
- Eliminating waste: waste is an activity that consumes time, resources or space but does not add any value to the product or service
- Reducing time: reducing the time needed to complete an activity from beginning to end is one of the most effective ways of eliminating waste and reducing costs
- Reducing total costs: a company should only produce based on customer requests given that overproduction increases a company's inventory costs.

The word "Lean" was coined for the first time by John Krafcik in his 1988 article, "Triumph of the Lean Production System", based on his Master's thesis at MIT Sloan School of Management. Krafcik had worked as a quality engineer in the joint venture between Toyota and GM NUMMI in California before attending MIT for his MBA studies. Krafcik's research was then continued by the International Motor Vehicle Program (IMVP) at MIT, and produced the international bestseller written by James P. Womack, Daniel Jones and Daniel Roos entitled "The Machine that Changed the World"[97].

14.5 Lean 4.0

In his recent research, Mayr[98] illustrates how the technologies of Industry 4.0 can contribute to the optimization of the methods and principles of Lean Manufacturing. Below, some Lean tools are listed and a brief description of how 4.0 technologies integrate with these concepts is provided.

Just in Time (JIT)

Just-in-Time aims to provide the right product at the right time in the quantity required. Here the main 4.0 tools are:

---

[97] Womack, J. P., Jones, D. T., & Roos, D. (2007). The machine that changed the world. Simon & Schuster

[98] Mayr A. et al, Lean 4.0 - A conceptual conjunction of lean management and Industry 4.0, 51st CIRP Conference on Manufacturing Systems, Procedia CIRP 72 (2018), pp 622-628, page 624.

- AGVs: they are used to move materials within a plant or warehouse, which are particularly beneficial in hazardous conditions
- IoT: extending Internet connectivity to any corporate asset helps to share information between the upstream and downstream stages of the process flow

Heijunka

The Japanese term Heijunka means leveling production to reduce overproduction, waste and to increase efficiency. Some of the 4.0 technologies that help achieve Heijunka are:

- Discrete Event Simulation: allows to analyze the behavior of a production system in order to optimize key metrics such as OEE, production costs, delivery times or to eliminate bottlenecks based on real data
- Big Data Analytics: the work planning phase can be optimized using historical data in combination with a better understanding of customer needs through an in-depth market analysis
- AGVs: as with JIT, they can help set up a production line

Kanban

The goal of the Kanban is to enable a continuous material flow while maintaining a predefined stock level to guarantee an uninterrupted material supply. Some of the main supporting 4.0 technologies are:

- Digital Twin: through simulation methods or real-time virtual representation of physical objects, the new Kanban loops can be planned with greater foresight and be perfectly integrated into the existing production environment
- IoT: it enables constant monitoring of the work in progress
- Cloud: information can be sent to the supply chain to extend the kanban loop to suppliers

Value Stream Mapping (VSM)

Value Stream Mapping is a graphical visualization method that aims to improve the transparency of the material flow and information within the value creation chain to identify waste. Some of the 4.0 technologies that come to our aid are:

- IoT: as for the Kanban, sensors and self-identification systems allow instant localization of objects and data analysis, facilitating the creation of a VSM
- Machine learning and data analysis support the design and optimization of the value flow. An optimized layout can even be automatically generated when the requirements are known.

Total Productive Maintenance (TPM)

It focuses on maintaining all equipment in the best working conditions to prevent breakdowns and delays in production processes. Some of the 4.0 tools to support the TPM are:

- Augmented Reality and Virtual Reality: they facilitate training and maintenance instructions. Furthermore, by viewing the virtual elements, operators can be guided remotely;
- With Machine Learning and Big Data analysis it is possible to analyze the correlation between the parameters of the conditions of the machinery and predict their probability of failure.

Single Minute Exchange of Die (SMED)

SMED aims to reduce uptime and inspection costs of set-up processes. SMED becomes even more effective when integrated with the following technologies:

- Virtual Reality: it can be used to train people to perform configuration operations in order to improve the learning curve;
- Augmented Reality: it supports the worker during set-up operations by displaying work instructions on a smart interface, such as glasses;
- Additive Manufacturing: in the case of finished products, the set-up time can be reduced to a minimum.

Visual Management (VM)

The purpose of Visual Management is to improve transparency by transferring objectives, standards and specifications into a visual representation. Part of Visual Management is the so-called 5S (sort, set in order, shine, standardize, sustain), a systematic approach to organize and improve workstation efficiency by standardization and arranging tools more effectively. The 4.0 tools to support VM and 5S are:

- IoT and Augmented Reality: systems equipped with RFID guarantee the identification and localization of objects. By means of special markers, augmented reality can also be used to subdivide work areas;
- Intelligent human-machine interface (HMI): tablets, smartphones, smart glasses and smartwatches can be used to show notifications to users in real time.

Poka-Yoke

The Japanese term Poka-Yoke, in English "mistake-proof", refers to all those mechanisms that help operators prevent errors. In this case, the most useful 4.0 tools are:

- IoT: systems equipped with RFID or NFC ensure correct identification, assignment and traceability of work batches in a plant

- Artificial intelligence and machine learning: plants and processes can self-adapt to guarantee optimal product quality
- Augmented Reality: as previously mentioned, it is vital in supporting workers through the use of work instructions on wearable devices

In the next Chapter we will explain how these principles and technologies must be exploited to implement an efficient and flexible production system.

14.6 Smart Factory and Lights-out manufacturing

In the last few years, the concept of light out manufacturing is become more and more popular. Factories that employ "lights-out manufacturing" are fully automated and require no human presence on-site. These factories are considered to be able to run "with the lights off." Many factories are capable of lights-out production, but few run exclusively lights-out.

In this sense, we can say that Smart Factories employ lights-out manufacturing; however, considering that the product variation is increasing due to mass personalization, additional solutions. Automation will not be the only trend to embrace, but smart technologies such as IoT, Big Data Analytics, IT Systems integration and Additive Manufacturing, just to mention some of them, must be implemented to enable a high level of self-reconfigurability.

Chapter 15: Smart Factory implementation

15.1 The 10-step process 283

15.2 Risks and associated challenges 295

15.3 Examples of Smart Factories 299

Chapter Summary

In this chapter we will look at the main steps in implementing a Smart Factory. An approach to reducing the risks associated with the design of such a production system will be described. However, it is not my goal to describe the steps to follow and the requirements to be met in a lot of detail. Instead, it will be the task of each team to identify and use the most appropriate methodologies and tools based on the specific requirements of their project. Finally, it should be noted that this approach does not follow a linear flow, but rather a series of loops. Going through one phase rather than another should be decided by the development team case by case.

Keywords: Smart Factory, Implementation

15.1 The 10-step process

An approach to reducing the risks associated with the design of such a production system will be described. However, it is not our goal to describe the steps to follow and the requirements to be met in a lot of detail. Instead, it will be the task of each team to identify and use the most appropriate methodologies and tools based on the specific requirements of their project.

Finally, it should be noted that this approach does not follow a linear flow, but rather a series of loops. Going through one phase rather than another should be decided by the development team case by case.

15.1.1 Defining the team

The first thing to do is to create a multidisciplinary team. Therefore, it is necessary to identify which skills are necessary for the development of our smart production system. Some key skills are:

1. Project Management
2. Research & Development
3. Product design
4. Process design
5. Production engineering

6. Supply chain

To these, we must add some skilled positions, traditionally not considered primary:

7. IT Expert
8. Data Scientist
9. Mechatronics Expert
10. Expert in Telecommunication Systems

15.1.2 Defining the requirements and constraints

As in any project, the requirements and design constraints must be identified. Therefore, it is necessary to have a clear understanding of the final corporate objective to be achieved at each level, as well as the constraints that are typically described in terms of:

- Quality
- Time
- Cost

15.1.3 Designing the system

The design of the production system represents the most critical part of the process. We can identify 6 main steps:

1. The first point is to identify the required production processes while maintaining a long-term vision of the

system. The vision should include an idea of which new products families will be designed and produced in the incoming years. This preliminary phase should include both product and process designers in order to:

- rethink the design of existing products, standardizing them in order to allow for the use of as few machines and tools as possible. This can lead to lower management and acquisition costs, better quality and shorter transportation time in the production lines. This phase is also called "Design for Manufacturing"

- identify which production technologies will generate a competitive advantage in the medium / long term. For example, let's imagine that a specific additive technology can be exploited in 5 years' time. What advantages could it introduce compared to our competitors? It will be necessary to take this into consideration during the investment phase and plan in the long-term. In this way, the capabilities required today and potential future gaps must be identified. This phase is called "Manufacturing for Design"

2. Once the product families have been identified, we can proceed with the definition of the production sequence;

3. Then, a make or buy analysis will be required in order to evaluate which processes should be kept in house and which it might be advisable to outsource;

4. Based on the processes that we have decided to outsource, it will be necessary to define the appropriate Supply Chain.

5. During this step, it will be necessary to think about how to arrange the assets, or to define the most appropriate production system, which will not necessarily be the final one. Typically, this occurs on the basis of the following variables:

    o Cost
    o Time
    o Quality
    o Flexibility

    Some options are:

    o Job-Shop: the machines are grouped by type of technological process. This gives flexibility to production, but normally a productivity level lower than a production line
    o Production line: consists of a sequence of operations optimized to facilitate continuous flow production at high volumes. Normally it guarantees high productivity, but low flexibility
    o Production cell: the work stations are organized to facilitate the continuous flow production of small batches

Generally, there is no better or worse production system. The final choice depends on your requirements. For example, a Job-Shop model is more flexible than a production line, which guarantees higher productivity at high volumes. Cell production, on the other hand, combines the advantages of the two approaches described, but it represents a trade-off.

6. After defining the sequence and the optimal production system, more details need to be defined, including:

    - Cycle time
    - Number of operators
    - Operator skills
    - Tools: type and quantity
    - Equipment: type and quantity
    - Setup times
    - Number of operators per setup
    - Type of productive asset: it can be a lathe, a milling machine, a robot, a testing machine, a plant, a work bench, etc.
    - Transfer method: AGVs, robots, trolleys, gantries, etc.
    - Transfer times from one station to another
    - Buffer strategy: FIFO, LIFO, etc.
    - Buffer size
    - MTBF: the average time between two failures (in English Mean Time Between Failure, or MTBF) is the time expected between intrinsic failures of a

mechanical or electronic system during normal system operation
- MTTR: (Mean Time to Repair) or average repair time is a basic measure of the maintainability of repairable items. It represents the average time needed to repair a faulty component or device
- Machine cost rate: is the annual depreciation cost divided by the total amount of hours of machine operation or expected operation
- Labor cost rate: this is the hourly cost rate for the various job tasks

These are just some of the factors that must be taken into account or evaluated through historical data. The collected values will then be analyzed in the next step by process simulation.

15.1.4 Simulating the system

Discrete Event Simulation (DES) models the functioning of a system as a discrete sequence of events over time. Each event occurs at a specific moment and marks a change of state in the system. It is not assumed that changes will occur in the system between consecutive events, therefore the simulation can jump directly in time from one event to another.

This type of simulation is a decision-making support tool often used to improve the understanding of interactions within the simulated system to identify possible problems.

According to Kokareva et al. (5), the main advantages include:

- increase in productivity of existing production plants up to 20%
- reduction of investments in planning new production plants up to 30%
- reduction of crossing times up to 40%
- optimization of system size, including buffer size
- reduction of investment risks through process validation
- optimization of production resources

Other advantages are:

- Identification of bottlenecks
- Estimate of investment costs (fixed) and management costs (variable)
- Balancing the production flow
- Estimate of the "What-if" scenarios

In order to design an optimized production system, iterative optimization loops must be carried out. These will likely have an impact on the initial decisions made in the previous phases.

There are several simulation software tools on the market. It is not my intention here to suggest one rather than another:

however, it must be said that their use requires specific skills that most companies do not have in house and must "acquire" or "rent".

15.1.5 Defining the production assets

Once the pre-established objectives have been reached in terms of productivity and flexibility, we can define the assets that must be supplied with more accuracy and detail. This stage could actually take several weeks or even months. The purchasing of a new asset may require validation at the supplier site, potential customizations and a subsequent negotiation phase. Without waiting for the successful completion of the acquisition phase, it is advisable to define at least the overall dimensions to start planning a layout.

15.1.6 Defining the layout

Similar to the previous points, this phase will also require several iterative loops. In fact, the layout could have a significant impact on the following aspects of previous simulations:

- Transportation time between processes
- Plant maintenance requirements (which constrain the space required)

Traditionally, the layout is defined using 2D CAD tools, but 3D CAD solutions are a standard nowadays. A 3D model system is also called a digital mock-up and leads to several advantages related to the reduction of associated risks:

- It is easier to evaluate the overall space
- It is possible to perform kinematic simulations, for example of robots
- Ergonomics simulations are possible
- Virtual Reality can be exploited
- A digital mock-up is the backbone of a Digital Twin

15.1.7 Simulating ergonomics

When a 3D model of the workstation is available, we are able to simulate and predict how its design impacts the operator's health. In fact, through specific software, it is possible to carry out ergonomics simulations in order to minimize hazards due to incorrect postures in the workstation. From the employer's point of view, the main advantage lies in protecting the health of their employees and consequently increasing productivity by reducing absences due to occupational diseases linked to incorrect postures.

15.1.8 Creating a proper IT Infrastructure

Once the assets have been defined, it's necessary to ensure that they are able to share the required information with a central system. Therefore, the next steps are:

- defining the hardware needed for each asset, such as integrated controls, sensors, wireless technologies, PLC
- predicting the type and quantity of data that will be exchanged
- sizing the IT infrastructure accordingly (transmission speed, computing power, server size)
- establishing adequate communication protocols

This phase must take place as soon as possible, once the necessary machinery has been identified. After that, all the information relating to the additional hardware required must be entered into Discrete Event Simulation to calculate the hourly cost of the system. If it is too high, it would be necessary to start again with iterative loops trying to reach the best trade-off.

In addition to the hardware for the implementation of Cyber-Physical Systems, it is necessary to create an IT architecture capable of collecting information and making it "flow" seamlessly at all company levels. Therefore, the following solutions should be implemented:

- Manufacturing Execution System (MES)

- Enterprise Resource Planning (ERP)
- Product Lifecycle Management (PLM)

Once the data collection method has been established, data scientists must implement algorithms in order to provide real-time feedback to the various production assets. Again, iterative loops must be performed to size the hardware and software.

15.1.9 Validating the system

To summarize, at this point we have:

- a set of simulations that show us if all the constraints have been considered and the requirements met
- the asset specifications
- the software specifications
- the system logic
- the factory layout in the form of a digital mock-up

To further reduce the risks and to be sure that the model created so far meets the company's requirements, it is recommended to use virtual reality.

From a practical point of view this consists of defining a workshop or "Virtual Event" in which the Management and Stakeholders have the opportunity to "experience" the production system by using virtual reality. This event can last for one or two days, depending on the size of the production system. The Assessment outcome will be a chart of initially defined requirements, on the basis of which the team and the Stakeholders will assess their fulfillment.

If changes are requested, the optimization loops will need to be restarted. The optimal result is usually achieved after 2 or 3 loops / workshops.

15.1.10 Digital Twin implementation

We now have the approval from the Management and we are ready to implement the designed production system. Once the assets have been installed, it will be necessary to conduct some tests to verify how information flows and to validate the algorithms implemented. It is easy to predict that it will hardly be satisfactory on the first attempt. Therefore, a debugging phase must be taken into account to identify potential issues. Moreover, keep in mind that the system set-up could still take a long time, although the risks have been minimized thanks to the precautions described in this book.

15.2 Risks and associated challenges

In the previous chapter, we briefly described the main benefits related to the implementation of a Smart Factory: a competitive edge generated by higher product and process quality in less time and lower production costs regardless of labor.

Flexibility, both in terms of product variety and throughput variation, will be the key factor for the years to come. Indeed, to remain competitive on the market, companies will have to satisfy the "voice of the customer" by customizing their products upon request. At the same time, automation will support processes by increasing productivity and quality, and reducing costs and delivery times. It will also free us from the need for low-cost labor.

However, all these benefits will not be "free of charge". In this chapter we will introduce some of the main risks and challenges you might face.

Standardization: the implementation of Industry 4.0 technologies implies the use of IT systems developed by different companies. In fact, the IT portfolio is constantly growing, as each department needs specialized software that is often difficult to integrate with other systems or platforms. In the same way, sensors and data transmission systems use protocols defined by the parent company, and yet these systems must be able to interface and exchange data. Protocol standardization could substantially simplify these activities. This would require an increasing number of developers to work together efficiently and allow companies to exploit the entire economic potential of Industry 4.0.

Cyber Security: one of the greatest risks within a Smart Factory is related to cyber security. In recent years, cyber-attacks against companies and individuals have increased steadily. Due to the lack of adequate data protection and security, these attacks have caused enormous financial damage. Production systems based on cyber-physical systems have therefore created the need for new security requirements.

IT infrastructure: another challenge in Industry 4.0 is the availability of an adequate IT infrastructure. The increased use of software and networking devices increases the dependence of companies on a powerful and scalable IT infrastructure. This implies the availability of adequate exchange, archiving and data processing systems.

Internet connection: an equally important problem is the availability of a reliable and fast internet connection: indeed, in the era of digitalization the state of "always staying connected" is an absolute must. An effective use of cyber-physical systems requires an infrastructure that allows for better and higher quality data exchange. In order to achieve low latency, high reliability, high quality and a complete broadband network, existing communication technologies must be improved.

System complexity: one of the main problems concerns the growing complexity within a Smart Factory. Due to the technological development over the last decades, the complexity of products and systems has already grown exponentially. Therefore, the complexity of production processes is also increasing considerably and will be less and less manageable in the absence of adequate technical and organizational countermeasures.

Organizational skills: the company organization plays a fundamental role: management must define a strategy and a well-structured plan for digitalization and demonstrate an understanding of IT systems and processes. In addition, organizational models must allow for a high level of cooperation and communication among all professionals. In order for employees to be prepared for new activities, the company must assume an active function with regards to managing change. Continuous training, changes in the organization of work and knowledge management will play a very important role in the future.

Financial Risks: the unwillingness to invest can be considered one of the main risks. In fact, investments in Industry 4.0 worldwide are currently still quite low. One of the problems lies in the lack of clarity of the added value that these technologies will bring both in the short and in the medium-long term. Long-term investments imply that the metalworking industries now have to evaluate which requirements products will have to meet in the future.

Unemployment: digitalization is replacing low added value activities and this is to be considered a side effect of the introduction of automation in industrial processes. However, it is not the first time that this has happened:

- with the agrarian revolution, animals replaced men
- the same happened with the steam engine during the first industrial revolution
- the effect was even more evident with the introduction of robots in the third industrial revolution

It is very likely that this will also happen with 4.0 technologies. One of the fundamental topics will be how to train employees: the required worker skills will change and being up-to-date on highly-demanded subjects such as mathematics and information technology will become more important than ever before. The same will happen with engineering subjects such as mechatronics and automation technology. Therefore, companies will have to develop an adequate continuous training plan for employees to ensure that the workers are at the cutting edge of technology.

15.3 Examples of Smart Factories

In this section we will illustrate three concrete examples of Smart Factories:

- Automation and integrated information flow: the BMW plant in Munich
- Process simulation: the new Boeing plant in Sheffield
- The Educational Factory: Factory 2050

15.3.1 Automation and integrated information flow: the BMW plant in Munich

Let's start with one of the most important brands in the automotive sector. The BMW plant in Munich is part of the Global Lighthouse Network, which is a network of 44 production sites. The network was selected out of more than 1000 sites by the Word Economic Forum as a point of reference for demonstrating the benefits of Industry 4.0.

About 8000 employees work in the factory, and approximately 1000 cars and over 2000 engines are produced every day, but the variety of products is such that only 2 cars per month are identical. The plant is located in a semi-central area of the city, so when it began to grow, it was no longer possible to expand the factory. For this reason, the only solution to increase the throughput was to create an advanced and streamlined system.

Figure 31: BMW Plant in Munich[99]

The manufacturing process starts with sheet metal pressing. The facility is able to produce about 35,000 components per day and operates over 3 shifts, full time, 7 days a week. Then, parts move on to the body shops where they are welded by approximately 1500 robots. The automation level here is 99%: only 30 minutes a day of downtime are dedicated to preventive maintenance. The complete investment cost was around 700 million Euros. Starting from the next step, the painting process, a greater level of vehicle customization begins. The newly inaugurated department is based on two

---

[99]

https://upload.wikimedia.org/wikipedia/commons/6/62/Conglomerado_B MW%2C_M%C3%BAnich%2C_Alemania_2012-04-28%2C_DD_02.JPG key concepts: sustainability and flexibility. In fact, the line consumes 25% less energy than the previous one and is able to work on a single piece flow by painting each model in any desired color. In the final assembly phase, all models and their variants are assembled on a single line of approximately 3 km in length. This process is almost entirely manual, although some phases of subassembly are still fully automated. What is worth mentioning here is the in-line inspection, in which machine learning, the cloud and Augmented Reality are integrated to verify the correct assembly of every component. The cycle time of a car is approximately 38 hours without compromising the quality in any way.

15.3.2 Process simulation: the new Boeing plant in Sheffield

In October 2018, Boeing opened its new factory in Sheffield, England. At full capacity, Boeing Sheffield will be able to produce thousands of parts per month, which will be assembled at the Boeing plant in Portland, United States. The plant currently produces more than 100 different types of actuators for Boeing 737 and 767. These actuators have the function of moving the flaps of the wing to provide greater lift at low speeds during take-off and landing[100].

---

[100]https://www.boeing.co.uk/news-media-room/news-releases/2018/october/boeing-opens-new-aircraft-part-factory-in-sheffield.page

The 6,200 square foot facility represents an investment of over £ 40 million, placing the world's largest aerospace company at the center of the corridor for global innovation in the city of Sheffield. The University of Sheffield, together with the Advanced Manufacturing Research Center, has developed a virtual simulation model of the new factory, which contributed to Boeing's goal of increasing productivity by up to 50%. Linking the virtual simulation model to Boeing's production data in real time, e.g. the delivery times of the material, the condition and maintenance of the machinery, as well as the planning of the processes will provide continuous advantages, such as:

- improving model accuracy
- real-time monitoring
- optimizing the production environment based on the latest factory simulation

"The use of the DES simulation gave Boeing a holistic view of the factory operations that will take place before the construction of Boeing Sheffield is completed."

Tim Underwood, Boeing.

15.3.3 The educational factory: Factory 2050

Why did Boeing decide to open its own plant in Sheffield? The University of Sheffield and the Advanced Manufacturing

Research Center are at the forefront of the development of new technologies, including 4.0 initiatives. In fact, there is another structure worthy of mention: Factory 2050[101].

Factory 2050 is the first educational factory in the UK dedicated entirely to collaborative research on assembly technologies, component manufacturing and digitally assisted reconfigurable processes. Factory 2050 was the first building to be completed on the University of Sheffield's new advanced production campus. The 6,730 sq m circular glass building houses the Integrated Manufacturing Group (IMG). Among their various activities, the group is developing models to meet the demand for high product variations and mass customization, as well as intelligent machines and processes to monitor and optimize their operations. They are also focusing on techniques to shorten delivery times, managing big data properly, as well as human-machine collaboration and assisted digital assembly techniques.

---

[101] https://www.amrc.co.uk/facilities/factory-2050

QUIZ PART 3

1) What is a Smart Factory?

1. A manufacturing facility which enable high level of automation in transaction processing and has real time analytics that helps in minimizing downtime and improving efficiency
2. An optimized manufacturing facility which is scalable enough to meet demand variation for existing products
3. A manufacturing facility which is able to produce parts with high level of standardization at very high volume

2) What are the benefits of high-volume personalization?

1. React quicky to customer tastes
2. Higher flexibility to satisfy customer requests
3. No need for assets upgrade

3) What are financial risks associated to a Smart Factory?

1. Industry 4.0 requires massive investments
2. Lack of transparency of economic added value
3. Companies generally don't recognize benefits of Industry 4.0

4) What is the main challenge regarding Organizational Skills?

1. People are not encouraged to learn new skills
2. Change Management is difficult
3. New organizational models are required
4. All of them

5) Which of the following statements are correct?

1. Industry 4.0 will increase complexity within a Smart Factory
2. Fast internet is not considered an issue within a Smart Factory
3. A comprehensive use of CPS requires an infrastructure that enables a better and higher quality data exchange
4. Change Management must start the highest hierarchy level
5. All of them

6) Why a Smart Factory can be defined also as a Human Factory, despite the potential loss of jobs?

1. Because low added value activities will be substituted by machines and workers will be dedicated to more valuable tasks
2. Because the Smart Factory will leverage the development of human skills

3. Because smart factories will have probably more workers, but working less hours
4. Because the Smart Factory will allow better interaction among workers
5. All of them

7) Put the 4 steps to implement a Smart Factory in the correct sequence

1. Implement a Digital Twin, effectively the connection between the physical and the real world
2. Prioritization of business units or product categories
3. Define the Real World, including the physical infrastructure and a smart production system
4. Define the Virtual World, including the IT system architecture and the required support for the real world

8) What are some of the main prerequisites to implement a Reconfigurable Manufacturing System?

1. Short / mid-term view on investments
2. Have a lifecycle perspective of the production system
3. Correlation between production system and new product portfolio and existence of product families
4. Specialistic production system overview
5. Structured approach to define the proper production system

6. All of them

9) What are some of the main benefits of a Digital Mockup?

1. It helps to assess ergonomic issues
2. It helps to assess HS&E risks associated with layouts
3. It helps to estimate the overall capital investment
4. It helps to identify bottlenecks
5. All of them

10) Why Multiphysics simulations are important for the implementation of Smart Factories?

1. To mitigate risks associated to special manufacturing and assembly processes
2. To replicate phenomena of the real world and simulate factory processes in a virtual environment
3. Both of them

Correct answers:

1) 1 **2)** 2 **3)** 2, 3, 4 **4)** 3 **5)** 2 **6)** 1, 3, 2, 4 **7)** 3 **8)** 2, 3 **9)** 1, 3, 4 **10)** 3

PART 4: REQUIREMENTS AND SKILLS IN DEMAND

In the previous chapter we described the principles of a Smart Factory and we suggest a structured approach for its implementation. This process should be driven by a series of defined requirements that organizations must put in place before starting this rewarding journey. Moreover, new soft and hard skills will be required: digitalization, multi-culturalism, communication, mechatronics and change management are only few of them.

List of chapters of Part 4

Chapter 16: Digital Transformation Requirements **312**

Chapter 17: Skills in demand **324**

Chapter 16: Digital Transformation Requirements

16.1 Develop a high-performance culture 313

16.2 Build Relevant Digital Capabilities 315

16.3 Attract Digital Talents 316

16.4 Develop a lifelong learning approach 317

16.5 Facilitate collaboration 319

16.6 Manage data as valuable asset 321

Chapter Summary

Digital technology plays a fundamental role in the implementation of smart factories; however, technology is not enough. Indeed, it's fundamental that organizations recognize the importance of critical requirements to be enabled. What are the main requirements that an organization needs to be developed to face up the digital transformation?

In this chapter, the most important ones will be presented.

Keywords: high-performance culture, digital capabilities, digital talents, lifelong learning

16.1 Develop a high-performance culture

"Winning Teams Winning Cultures"[102] is a masterpiece I strongly recommend. The book was written by Larry Senn and Jim Hart who are Chairman and President (and CEO) of Senn Delaney, a Heidrick & Struggles company, which was the first firm in the world to focus exclusively on transforming cultures. The book helps to explain why a team made up of highly competent, knowledgeable and committed leaders can still be ineffective, or why two companies in the same industry, with similar strategies, equipment and pricing achieve such different results.

The main objective of the book is to explain how to implement the right culture inside a company in order to achieve success. And to do that the book focuses on a very important word: Change. It is easier to decide on change than get people to change!

Indeed, people and organizations are creatures of habit, and changing habits is much harder than changing structures or systems. The authors call this phenomenon "the jaws of culture" because cultural habits, such as resistance to change and turf issues, chew up the improvement process and reduce the results. Most change initiatives continue to focus almost exclusively on the operational and technical side and too often

---

[102] Larry Senn, Jim Hart, Winning Teams Winning Cultures, Second Edition, 2014

they ignore the human or behavioral side of change. If you have ever tried to make changes or implement improvement initiatives in an unreceptive culture, you know it is like trying to swim against the current: you put a lot of effort but don't make much forward progress.

The importance of aligning strategy and culture was stated well in a Business Week article: *"A corporation's culture can be its greatest strength when it is consistent with its strategies. But a culture that prevents a company from meeting competitive threats, or from adapting to changing economic or social environments, can lead to the company's stagnation and ultimate demise"* – Business Week

Or, again: *"Culture eats strategy for breakfast"* – Sign in the "war room" of Ford Motor Company

What are the main barriers in developing a high-performance culture? Here some:

- Internal competition between business units and functions -"we-they" attitudes
- Lack of agility or ability to quickly adapt
- Hierarchical top-down tendencies and boss-driven leadership style
- Bureaucratic tendencies and lack of innovation
- An "observer-critic" culture that kills new ideas
- Entitlement mindset and poor empowerment
- Lack of accountability
- Trust issues

- Inability to foster and support diversity of ideas and people
- Conflict avoidance and polite, but passive-aggressive, behaviors

16.2 Build Relevant Digital Capabilities

Industry 4.0 is based on a set of technologies, mainly digital, which enable to achieve the company's objectives. Therefore, it is important that organizations develop internal digital capabilities and learn how to use and exploit even external digital sources. This is even more true at middle and top management level. Indeed, lack of digital competences goes in parallel with the seniority level. On the other hand, is at the high seniority level that important decisions on investments are taken.

In this sense, young employees will play a more important role within organizations as they will be the driver of digital transformation. For this reason, it is important that they will be self-conscious of the impact and the new vital lymph they can bring with them.

16.3 Attract Digital Talents

As just said, it is fundamental that companies will be able to attract people with digital skills or willing to learn how to use digital tools. Indeed, smart devices and technologies are going to be spread up at all different organization level:

Shopfloor
- Work instructions will be potentially displayed on smartphones wrapped on an arm, or on tablets, touchscreen, or even on smart glasses by using Augmented Reality
- Tools, Fixtures, Masks and a lot of other potential applications can be made by Additive Manufacturing techniques
- Workers will learn how to collaborate with collaborative robots
- They will learn how to find assets by checking a smartphone as well by using Real Time Locating Systems (RTLS)

Product Design and Development: at this level, digital tools have been pretty much well widespread already. For example, simulation tools like CAD modeling, Finite Element Analysis and Multiphysics Modeling techniques are well-known by most of design departments. What is still probably not so well known is how to use 3D printers or Virtual Reality to support the design phase; factories and production cells will be simulated to mitigate risks by using Discrete Event Simulation software. The University of Sheffield Advanced Manufacturing Research Centre (AMRC) has developed a virtual simulation model of the new Boeing Sheffield facility. The model will help to validate the opportunities Boeing has to increase productivity by up to 50 per cent.

Data-Driven Decision Making: data-driven decision making involves making decisions that are backed up by hard data rather than making decisions that are intuitive or based on observation alone. As business technology has advanced exponentially in recent years, data-driven decision making has become a much more fundamental part of all sorts of industries, including important fields like medicine, transportation and equipment manufacturing. Internet of Things (IoT), Cloud Computing, Big Data Analytics and Artificial Intelligence will provide the right support to collect real-time data, analyze them and provide recommendation by using algorithms.

16.4 Develop a lifelong learning approach

Lifelong learning can be defined as the ongoing, voluntary and self-motivated pursuit of knowledge for either personal or professional reasons. Nowadays, lifelong learning is not just an option. Indeed, rapid changes of technologies and shifting in priorities are moving faster than ever, and it is still essential to keep ourselves updated. The just digitalization trend is just one example.

Accenture and the Manufacturing Institute surveyed more than 300 US manufacturing companies in 2013 and 2014, it was found that 80% of these companies invest in employees with training programs spending on average $1,000 annually per employee[103].

Luckily, opportunities are not missing. Some of them include:

- **Workshops:** events in which technical qualifications and skills are reinforced and developed. Workshops can be used to train both technical and personal qualifications and skills. Whereas workshops can deal with almost any technical topic, they are also well-suited and commonly used to deliver soft skills, for example about self-management, teamwork, and effective business communications.
- **Professional Development Courses:** they are a very effective measure reinforcing technical and personal skills. They have specific content and can be tailored to exact needs.
- **MOOC:** it stands for Massive Open Online Course and it is an online course aimed at unlimited participation and open access via the web. In addition to traditional course materials such as filmed lectures, readings, and problem

---

[103] http://www.themanufacturinginstitute.org/Research/Skills-and-Training-Study/~/media/70965D0C4A944329894C96E0316DF336.ashx

sets, many MOOCs provide interactive courses with user forums to support community interactions among students, professors, and teaching assistants as well as immediate feedback to quick quizzes and assignments. MOOCs are a recent and widely researched development in distance education which were first introduced in 2006 and emerged as a popular mode of learning in 2012.

16.5 Facilitate collaboration

Industry 4.0 goes beyond internal manufacturing. The increasing connection of companies with third parties along the value chain creates the need for alliances and interoperability standards. It is therefore clear that collaboration within and among different organizations, in national and international environments, must be strengthen. How?

- **Seek alliances and strategic partnerships**: businesses that apparently don't have nothing to share, now are going to create partnerships and collaborations. Moreover, a variety of competences that new business scenario will lead, will be unlikely available within the same organization. The decision by Apple and Google to enter the automotive market shows that a tech company can now transform into a car company.

- **Get involved in the definition of standards**: this is a typical problem when new technologies are developed and then massively used until to become a standard. Therefore, it becomes clear how important is to establish the right standard in order that systems can communicate and interact.

"It is precisely this objective which motivated the German industrial associations BITKOM, VDMA and ZVEI, together with the standards organizations DIN and DKE, to set up the Standardization Council Industrie 4.0 (SCI 4.0) [...]. The SCI 4.0 is responsible for orchestrating standardization activities and, in this role, acts as a point of contact in connection with all matters relating to standardization in the context of Industrie 4.0. It brings German stakeholders together and represents their interests in international bodies and consortia"[104]

Key element of the Standardization Roadmap is the role that humans play in "smart factories". The document also addresses the harmonization of smart manufacturing components, reference and data models in Industrie 4.0, as well as communication technologies, service robotics and legal issues. Experts from the areas of business, research, science and politics have contributed to the development of the Roadmap. The Roadmap for Industrie

---

[104] GERMAN STANDARDIZATION ROADMAP Industrie 4.0 Version 3, DIN e. V., 2018

4.0 is a "living" document that is continually being developed by DIN and DKE, who are also responsible for publishing it. Anyone interested in Industry 4.0 is welcome to participate in this work.

16.6 Manage data as valuable asset

Data is the new gold. By using Big Data and Analytics techniques such as statistics, machine learning, organizations can mine hidden data and provide benefits without precedents:

- **Data-Driven Decision Making**: Data mining techniques such as statistics or machine learning can extract useful information from raw data to support the decision-making process. Indeed, data-driven decision making is far more reliable and powerful than just simply opinions

- **Understanding and Targeting Consumers**: since marketing is all about reaching the right customers at the right time, Big Data Analytics can be used to predict purchases, analyze customer behaviour. The "you may also like" approach widely use now in almost all e-commerce platform is an example of consumers targeting

- **Self-optimization**: through machine learning, systems can adapt, optimize and improve themselves to achieve better performances

- **Security**: Cyber-security will have massive benefits in using data analytics techniques. IBM's fraud detection technology helped a large global money-transfer company stop more than $37 million in fraud[105]

- **Smart Factories:** Big Data Analytics is the brain of a Smart Factory: through IoT and CPS, raw data are collected (in the Cloud) and then analyzed through data mining techniques to improve performances

- **Smart Product Development:** Smart Product Development is the fostering of Industry 4.0 technologies to improve all different stages in the product development process, independently from the method, approach or specific process selected

---

[105] https://dataflog.com/read/using-big-data-to-improve-law-enforcement/3485

Chapter 17: Skills in demand

17.1 Hard Skills 325
17.2 Soft Skills 330

Chapter Summary

In this final chapter, main hard and soft skills will be described: indeed, although new technical capabilities are considered a must, however is it important to highlight the fundamental role of soft skills to allow the new approach to work to run smoothly.

Hard skills are specific, teachable abilities that can be defined and measured, such as typing, writing, math, reading and the ability to use software programs. By contrast, soft skills are less tangible and harder to quantify, such as etiquette, getting along with others, listening and engaging in small talk.

Keywords: mechatronics & automation, production & processes, materials, computer technology, data science, change management, creativity, socialization, collaboration, multi-disciplinary, adaptability, multi-culturalism

The demand for technical talents will drive the shift of job creation within organizations.

More specifically, the manufacturing industry will require skilled employees to develop and run advanced manufacturing tools and systems and analyze data received from machines, consumers and global resources. This results in a rinsing need for skilled workers trained in cross-functional areas and with capabilities to manage new processes. As this is key to success of innovative and smart organizations, the role of human factor will increase significantly[106].

Giving the increasing rate of change of technologies, the fourth industrial revolution will demand and place more emphasis on the ability of workers to adapt continuously and learn new skills and approaches within a variety of contexts.

17.1 Hard Skills

Mechatronics & Automation

Mechatronics generally involves mechanical and electronic engineering; robots designed therein tend to have physical purposes. They may be made for automation, they may not.

---

[106] Gehrke L. et al, A Discussion of Qualifications and Skills in the Factory of the Future: A German and American Perspective, VDI and ASME, April 2015

Automation is geared towards completing repetitive tasks; however, this is not limited to mechanical solutions.

Made this premise, these skills became increasingly important with the rise of the third industrial revolution, as discussed in chapter 1. With the fourth industrial revolution, these skills become even more fundamental.

Production & Processes

Smart factories will exploit digital technologies massively. However, it is fundamental that they are used wisely. For example, autonomation is one of the pillars of lean systems, along with waste reduction and Just-In-Time manufacturing. By deploying smart, flexible automation in manufacturing processes, manufacturers can help improve product flow and quality while improving factory equipment uptime.

However, automation is not the end goal. The end goal is to deliver products or services at the desired cost, at the right time, with the right quality.

Single steps in the manufacturing process will definitely have benefits from new technologies, but it is still fundamental that a holistic approach must be kept.

In this sense, production & processes skills will be becoming more important in the next years. For example, a mechatronic engineer can develop a specific robot to perform an operation with high quality and high efficiency (how), but it is the process engineer who identifies the task (what and where).

Materials

New technologies lead to new materials. Material science is evolving systematically through the time. The first and the second industrial revolutions were possible with the rise of steel industry: the supply of cheaper iron and steel aided a number of industries, such as those making nails, hinges, wire and other hardware items. The development of machine tools allowed better working of iron, causing it to be increasingly used in the rapidly growing machinery and engine industries. Then, new materials such as ceramics and composites supported the increasing of performances:

- Ceramics increased the power and efficiency of jet engines
- Composites (e.g. carbon fiber and glass fiber) made products stiffer and lighter
- Semiconductors made possible the computer revolution (3rd industrial revolution)
- Superconductors are revolutionizing applications like electric grid, cell phone technology and medical diagnosis

Additive Manufacturing (AM) will benefit enormously from material science and it opened new frontiers to be explored.

Computer Technology

Based on the fact that most of the key technologies of Industry 4.0 implies the use of digital technologies, it becomes evident how this skill will have e growing importance in the future. Internet of Things will connect Cyber-Physical-Systems through sensors using different types of standard and protocol, organizations will be highly integrated internally and externally and communication must flow smoothly. Digital systems / platform / software that now are most of the time standalone will be connected in a network (or cloud). The IT infrastructure will be significantly different due to the increasing amount of data (Big Data) to be exchanged and the consequent increasing amount of data storage required. Moreover, higher computational power will be required to allow data scientist to run tools to extract strategic data. All these challenges (IT system integration, data exchange, data storage and data analytics) will need high demand of computer technology skills.

Data Science

Being a Data Scientist implies having a high-level education (Master or PhD) in technical fields. The most common fields of study are Mathematics and Statistics (32%), followed by Computer Science (19%) and Engineering (16%). A degree in any of these courses will give you the skills you need to process and analyze big data[107].

Another important aspect is the knowledge of some of the most powerful analytical tools:

- **Python Coding:** Python is the most common coding language I typically see required in data science roles, along with Java, Perl, or C/C++. Python is a great programming language for data scientists. This is why 40 percent of respondents surveyed by O'Reilly use Python as their major programming language.
- **SQL Database Coding:** SQL (structured query language) is a programming language that can help you to carry out operations like add, delete and extract data from a database. It can also help you to carry out analytical functions and transform database structures.
- **Apache Spark:** Apache Spark is becoming the most popular big data technology worldwide. Apache Spark is specifically designed for data science to help run its complicated algorithm faster. It helps in disseminating data processing when you are dealing with a big sea of data thereby, saving time.

---

[107] https://www.kdnuggets.com/2018/05/simplilearn-9-must-have-skills-data-scientist.html

17.2 Soft Skills

Change Management

Change Management is a systematic approach to dealing with the transition or transformation of an organization's goals, processes or technologies. The purpose of change management is to implement strategies for effecting change, controlling change and helping people to adapt to change. It is important to spread a Change Management culture within the organization to exploit opportunities from Industry 4.0. Change Management is faced with the fundamental difficulties of integration and navigation, and human factors. Change Management must also take into account the human aspect where emotions and how they are handled play a significant role in implementing change successfully. One of the major factors which block the change management process is people's natural tendency for inertia. Just as in Newton's first law of motion, people are resistant to change in organisations because it means to move out from the "comfort zone".

The notion of doing things this way, because 'this is the way we have always done them', can be particularly hard to overcome, but at the same time, dangerous.

"That's why a man's fortunes may change: because the times change, but he does not change his approach" N. Machiavelli, Il Principe

To assist with this, a number of models have been developed which help identify their readiness for change and then to recommend the steps through which they could move.

As Change Management becomes more necessary in the business cycle of organizations, it is beginning to be taught as its own academic disciple at universities. There is a growing number of universities with research units dedicated to the study of organizational change.

Creativity

Cognitive abilities and complex problem solving will be far more in demand than content skills. Indeed, we learned already how one of the biggest challenges dealing with Industry 4.0 is complexity. Creativity will be highly in demand. Data scientists, for example, will require a high dose of creativity to understand how to mine Big Data and collect useful information to identify, for example, the root cause of a problem. At the same time, creativity must be used by product development teams once that manufacturing constraints don't exist anymore due to the freedom allowed by new techniques like Additive Manufacturing. And again, cybersecurity experts must be creative to understand new possible way to keep IT safe from cyber threats. Digital technologies are shapeless, which means that new threats and opportunities are now possible and it is up to creativity people to find them.

Socialization

Modern lifestyle has negative impact on our interpersonal communication behaviour: time has become the most precious resource, and people are finding means of saving time because of their fast paced life, social media has become a preferred medium for communication with the proliferation of digital and mobile technologies, digitalization has reduced the face to face interaction of human beings whether it is for marketing or promoting a product or a personal communication and he mobile phone has created a social situation whereby people are getting used to avoidance of person to person communication by switching over to mobile. It is a paradox, but digital technologies with higher potential of interaction led people to develop fewer social skills. On the other hand, fundamental activities required by high-performing teams like brainstorming sessions, team meetings and everyday tasks require a high level of human interaction. Social skills like empathy (the ability to understand and share the feelings of another) and emotional intelligence (the capacity to be aware of, control, and express one's emotions, and to handle interpersonal relationships judiciously and empathetically) will be fundamental but hard to find in the context we just described.

Collaboration

People must be able to collaborate in a high challenging but even more stimulating scenario. Virtual Teams, for example, are made by people located in different buildings, cities, countries or continents. They may be part of the same organization or they may come from different companies. A collateral skill required to work with virtual teams is the linguistic knowledge. English, for example, is not an option anymore for a lot of jobs where only few years ago was not required. To be able to exploit the knowledge of people and all around the world, it is fundamental to develop enough linguistic capability.

Multi-disciplinary

We live in a multifaceted world and everybody with at least 10 years of experience have easily noted how jobs have changed since they started. For example, manual drawings turned to 3D CAD modeling, paper letters turned into email, paper work instructions turned into touch screen monitors and manual lathes turned into CNC machines. In the Industry 4.0 scenario, this will become even more extreme. In the previous sections, we highlighted how hard skills that are sensibly different from each other are effectively required to develop smart factory. Which means also that each expert should have a minimum of understanding of different subjects: the big data scientist, for example, should understand requirements from a process expert to improve a machining operation, and a material expert should understand how additive manufacturing works to understand related problems to be solved. Of course, this is true vice versa as well.

Multi-culturalism

Working in virtual teams with people having different skills implies dealing with people with different multiple backgrounds. For example, Germans, Americans and Chinese have a different approach to solving problems, but it doesn't mean that one is better than another. If you had the opportunity to live and work outside your hometown, even only few kilometers, you would have certainly noted that behaviors are different. Therefore, it is easy to understand that differences experienced in multi-disciplinary multi-skilled and multi-cultural environments requires a high level of adaptability and flexibility. In this sense, personal international experiences and university exchange programs will be considered in the future much more valuable than other previously better considered skills.

Personal adaptability

Being flexible to work with different people, facing with different subjects and dealing with cultures will be not enough. Indeed, people should be able to adapt themselves to impacts that new technologies will lead to our lives. Being flexible and adaptable to new changes will be not just a nice-to-have, but rather a must requirement.

QUIZ PART 4

1) What is «the jaws of culture»? Choose the correct answer:

1. It is a phenomenon which explains why changing structures or systems is much harder than changing habits
2. It is a phenomenon which explains why changing habits is much harder than changing structures or systems
3. It is a phenomenon which helps to change habits

2) According to your experience, what are the top 5 cultural barriers?

3) At which company level is more important to develop digital capabilities?

1. At operational level, because people must utilize new technologies every day
2. At mid management level, because they must convince high-level management to invest in new technologies and at the same time organize workers at operation level

3. At higher level, because the Management must recognize the positive impacts and therefore plan investments

4) What are the main levers to develop digital capabilities?

1. Lifelong learning approach
2. Attract digital talents
3. Collaboration with universities and research centers
4. Use public incentives

5) In which main areas can digital capabilities be relevant?

1. New Product Development
2. Operations
3. Data driven decision making
4. Supply Chain
5. All of them

6) Why a lifelong learning approach is important?

1. Because academic knowledge is not enough to follow upcoming trends and skills are always evolving
2. Because certifications are fundamental to improve in the career path
3. Because technology is continuously evolving, while people skills don't improve accordingly

7) What are hard skills?

1. Skills that can be acquired only through an academic degree
2. Skills that are fundamental to acquire for a specific job or task
3. Skills that are difficult to acquire

8) What are some of the main hard skills in demand?

1. Materials
2. Personal Flexibility
3. Project Management
4. Production & processes
5. Data Science
6. Finance
7. Computer Technology
8. Mechatronics & Automation

9) What are soft skills?

1. A set of skills associated with personal and social factors
2. A set of skills that are easy to acquire
3. A set of skills which are nice to have but not fundamental in a working environment

10) What are some of the main soft skills in demand?

1. Change Management
2. Computer Technology
3. Multi-culturalism
4. Collaboration
5. Socialization
6. Coding
7. Creativity

Correct answers:

1) 2   **3)** 3   **4)** 1, 2, 3   **5)** 5   **6)** 1, 3   **7)** 2   **8)** 1, 4, 5, 7, 8   **9)** 1   **10)** 1, 3, 4, 5, 7

Conclusion

We arrived at the end of this journey. I hope you found the material of this book interesting and it fulfilled your expectation.

Industry 4.0 was born 10 years ago, and nevertheless most of the manufacturing companies have only begun to embrace this trend. The aerospace and automotive industries, historically at the forefront of technology, were the first industries to implement new digital solutions, both to improve performance and to reduce the costs of product / process development with the aim of improving their competitiveness. Moreover, competitiveness becomes a crucial aspect in the globalized world. Together with the aerospace and automotive giants, also small and medium-sized enterprises have begun to approach new technologies, both thanks to the different types of support that the industrial countries have put in place in the meantime, and to the global pandemic that has accelerated the digital transformation.

Finally, the implementation costs associated to new technologies are becoming more and more accessible over the years. However, the main barriers to renew the production systems in industrialized countries are mainly cultural rather than technological and economic. Global competition and the rapid change in society are forcing to adopt an attitude of continuous innovation and for this reason we need adopt a lifelong learning approach to increase our knowledge and use the right tools.

The goal of this book was precisely this: to provide a practical and concrete set of information to managers and engineers within manufacturing organizations.

What's next?

The next step will be probably the most challenging but at the same time exciting: the implementation of a new approach. For this, the knowledge about Industry 4.0 should be spread all over the company and the supply chain and pilot projects should be implemented on a small scale in order to proof the effectiveness of new solutions even to the most skeptical people. As we already said several times in this book, this will be not just an option anymore, but a matter of surviving and being more competitive in the future scenarios of an unpredictable-globalized world.

List of References

- Andersen et al, Prerequisites and Barriers for the Development of Reconfigurable Manufacturing Systems for High Speed Ramp-up, 3rd International Conference on Ramp-up Management (ICRM), Procedia CIRP 51 (2016) 7 – 12
- Barnatt C, A Brief Guide to Cloud Computing: An essential guide to the next computing revolution. (Brief Histories) Little, Brown Book Group. Kindle Edition, 2010
- Barnatt C., 3D Printing: Second Edition, CreateSpace Independent Publishing Platform, 2014
- Bejlegaard M et al, Reconfigurable Manufacturing Potential in Small and Medium Enterprises with Low Volume and High Variety, 3rd International Conference on Ramp-up Management (ICRM), Procedia CIRP 51 (2016), 32–37
- Franco L, Arrivano i robot e non solo in fabbrica. Ecco che cosa dovremmo fare perchè non ci rubino il lavoro, from FQ Millennium Magazine, Nov 2017
- Gandolfi E, Handbook of Research on K-12 Online and Blended Learning (2nd ed.), Publisher: ETC Press, Editors: Kennedy, K, Ferdig, R.E., pp.545-561
- Gates, Mark. Blockchain: Ultimate guide to understanding blockchain, bitcoin, cryptocurrencies, smart contracts and the future of money. Kindle Edition.

- Gehrke L. et al, A Discussion of Qualifications and Skills in the Factory of the Future: A German and American Perspective, VDI and ASME, April 2015
- GERMAN STANDARDIZATION ROADMAP Industrie 4.0 Version 3, DIN e. V., 2018
- Grieves M, Digital Twin: Manufacturing Excellence through Virtual Factory Replication, March 2015
- Herrmann F, The Smart Factory and its risks, Systems 2018, 6, 38; doi:10.3390/systems6040038
- http://www.arcam.com/company/about-arcam/history/
- http://www.themanufacturinginstitute.org/Research/Skills-and-Training-Study/~/media/70965D0C4A944329894C96E0316DF336.ashx
- https://ark-invest.com/articles/analyst-research/industrial-robot-cost-declines/
- https://blog.robotiq.com/collaborative-robot-ebook
- https://commons.m.wikimedia.org/wiki/File:Binder_jetting.png
  https://commons.wikimedia.org/wiki/File:Selective_laser_melting_system_schematic.jpg
- https://commons.wikimedia.org/wiki/File:3D_Printer_Extruder.png
- https://commons.wikimedia.org/wiki/File:Blockchain-Process.png
- https://commons.wikimedia.org/wiki/File:Drone_First_Test_Flight.jpg

- https://commons.wikimedia.org/wiki/File:Global_Revenue_from_Smart_Wearables_and_hearables.png
- https://commons.wikimedia.org/wiki/File:Half_filled_server_racks.jpg
- https://commons.wikimedia.org/wiki/File:Industry_4.0.png
- https://commons.wikimedia.org/wiki/File:Inkjet_3D_Printing.svg
- https://commons.wikimedia.org/wiki/File:Ramahololens.jpg
- https://commons.wikimedia.org/wiki/File:Stereolithography_apparatus_vector.svg
- https://commons.wikimedia.org/wiki/File:Tangleimage.jpg
- https://datafloq.com/read/using-big-data-to-improve-law-enforcement/3485
- https://en.wikipedia.org/wiki/Quadcopter
- https://investing.curiouscatblog.net/2011/12/28/chart-of-manufacturing-output-from-2000-to-2010-by-country/
- https://it.m.wikipedia.org/wiki/File:Clark%27s_Sector_model.png
- https://www.additivemanufacturing.media/articles/am-101-hybrid-manufacturing
- https://www.amrc.co.uk/facilities/factory-2050
- https://www.audi-mediacenter.com/en/press-releases/audi-uses-drones-to-locate-vehicles-at-neckarsulm-site-

- 12999#:~:text=The%20specially%20developed%20hexacopter%2C%20a,of%20the%20cars%20parked%20there.
- https://www.bangkokbankinnohub.com/digitaltwin/
- https://www.boeing.co.uk/news-media-room/news-releases/2018/october/boeing-opens-new-aircraft-part-factory-in-sheffield.page
- https://www.businessinsider.com/elon-musk-universal-basic-income-2017-2
- https://www.datasciencecentral.com/profiles/blogs/difference-of-data-science-machine-learning-and-data-mining
- https://www.economist.com/business/2016/12/03/siemens-and-general-electric-gear-up-for-the-internet-of-things
- https://www.eetimes.com/author.asp?section_id=36&doc_id=1330462
- https://www.forbes.com/sites/timworstall/2016/10/03/us-wages-have-been-rising-faster-than-productivity-for-decades/#43540eac7342
- https://www.investopedia.com/articles/investing/020515/business-google.asp
- https://www.kdnuggets.com/2018/05/simplilearn-9-must-have-skills-data-scientist.html
- https://www.kdnuggets.com/2018/05/simplilearn-9-must-have-skills-data-scientist.html
- https://www.newgenapps.com/blog/augmented-reality-technology-how-ar-works
- https://www.ofcom.org.uk/__data/assets/pdf_file/0031/19498/2014_uk_cmr.pdf

- https://www.simplilearn.com/data-science-vs-data-analytics-vs-machine-learning-article
- https://www.theguardian.com/technology/2018/jan/31/amazon-warehouse-wristband-tracking
- https://www.themarketingtechnologist.co/virtual-reality-connecting-unity-to-the-cave/
- https://www.youtube.com/watch?app=desktop&v=otE6CnFUXDA
- Kacperczyk, Marcin; Neuefeind, Marvin. Cryptocurrency - A Trader's Handbook: A Complete Guide on How to Trade Bitcoin and Altcoins. Kindle Edition.
- Kagermann H., Lukas W-D., Wahlster W., Industrie 4.0: Mit dem Internet der Dinge auf dem Weg zur 4. industriellen Revolution, 2011
- Kokareva V.V. et al, Production Processes Management by Simulation in Tecnomatix Plant Simulation, Applied Mechanics and Materials Vol 756 (2015) pp 604-609
- Larry Senn, Jim Hart, Winning Teams Winning Cultures, Second Edition, 2014
- Marsh P., The New Industrial Revolution: Consumers, Globalization and the End of Mass Production, Yale University Press publications, 2012
- Meeuwisse R, "Cybersecurity for Beginners", Cyber Simplicity Ltd; 2nd edition (March 14, 2017)
- Padhi N, Setting up a Smart Factory (Industry 4.0)-A Practical Approach, Nov, 2018

- Pereira A.C., Romero F, "A review of the meanings and the implications of the Industry 4.0 concept", Procedia Manufacturing, Volume 13, 2017, Pages 1206-1214
- Raja Wasim Ahmada et al, Blockchain for Aerospace and Defense: Opportunities and Open Research Challenges, Computers & Industrial Engineering Journal, November 2020
- Rauch E, Dallasega P, Matt D T, The way from Lean Product Development (LPD) to Smart Product Development (SPD), 26th CIRP Design Conference, Procedia CIRP 50 (2016) 26 – 31
- Research Report: The State of IoT Adoption in Product Development 2019, Engineering.com, 2019
- Romandini M, Condannato da un legale che sembra un tostapane, from FQ Millennium Magazine, Nov 2017
- Schwab K, The Fourth industrial Revolution, Portfolio Penguin, 2016
- Stratasys white paper, 3D PRINTING JIGS & FIXTURES FOR THE PRODUCTION FLOOR
- Unmanned Aircraft Systems Roadmap. Archived from the original (PDF) on 2 October 2008.
- Wang B, The Future of Manufacturing: a new perspective, Engineering Volume 4, Issue 5, October 2018, Pages 722-728
- Wangler B., Paheerathan S J, Horizontal and vertical integration of organizational IT systems, Information Systems Engineering, The Pennsylvania State University, 2000

List of Figures

Figure 1: Book framework.. XII
Figure 2: The Four Industrial Revolutions 11
Figure 3: Manufacturing Production by Country 19
Figure 4: Clark's sector Model in the US................................ 20
Figure 5: Disconnect between productivity and typical worker's compensation from 1948 to 2014 in the US 22
Figure 6: The five stages of production 27
Figure 7: The 9 Key Technologies, according BCG 34
Figure 8: Industrial robot cost decline 68
Figure 9: A drone... 82
Figure 10: FDM 3D Printer Extruder 94
Figure 11: How Photopolymerization works 98
Figure 12: Schematic representation of Inkjet Technology 100
Figure 13: How Binder Jetting works 102
Figure 14: How Laser Sintering works.................................. 105
Figure 15: Example of 3D printed support for final inspection 116
Figure 16: Microsoft HoloLens Headset............................... 142
Figure 17: Pictorial representation of CAVE technology 153
Figure 18: HTC Vive Headset... 156
Figure 19: Storage supply and demand from 2006 to 2020 163
Figure 20: Explosion of digital data from 2006 to 2020...... 164
Figure 21: Levels of Data Science... 169
Figure 22: Service models in Cloud Computing 185

Figure 23: Server Racks 193
Figure 24: Block scheme of a Discrete Event Simulation process steps 204
Figure 25: Vertical and Horizontal integration under Industry 4.0 212
Figure 26: Global Revenue from Smart Wearables and Hearables 236
Figure 27: concept representation of a Digital Twin 244
Figure 28: How blockchain works 248
Figure 29: Organization of Tangle blocks............................ 251
Figure 30: Pictorial representation of a Smart Factory and its technologies... 266
Figure 31: BMW Plant in Munich 300

List of Tables

Table 1: ABB IRB 1400 Yumi Data Sheet 77
Table 2: Comau Aura Data Sheet 78
Table 3: Fanuc CE 35iA Data Sheet 79
Table 4: Kuka LBR IIWA 14 R820 Data Sheet 80
Table 5: Universal Robots UR3 / U5 Data Sheets.................. 81
Table 6: Material Extrusion VS Photopolymerization 99
Table 7: How DES can support different phases in manufacturing.. 202

Printed in Great Britain
by Amazon